GREAT GAMES FOR YOUNG PEOPLE

Marilee A. Gustafson, MA
Sue K. Wolfe
Cheryl L. King
Anoka Senior High School
Anoka, Minnesota

Human Kinetics Books
Champaign, Illinois

Library of Congress Cataloging-in-Publication Data

Gustafson, Marilee A., 1947-
  Great games for young people / Marilee A. Gustafson, Sue K. Wolfe,
Cheryl L. King.
    p.   cm.
  Includes index.
  ISBN 0-87322-299-7
  1. Physical education for children. 2. Games. I. Wolfe, Sue K.,
1954-   . II. King, Cheryl L., 1948-   . III. Title.
  GV443.G85   1991
  613.7'042--dc20   90-38917

ISBN: 0-87322-299-7

Acquisitions Editor: Rick Frey, PhD
Developmental Editor: Kathy Kane; Production Editor: Valerie Hall; Assistant Editors: Julia Anderson, Dawn Levy, Timothy Ryan; Copyeditor: Wendy Nelson; Proofreader: Claire Huisman; Production Director: Ernie Noa; Typesetter: Brad Colson; Text Design: Keith Blomberg; Text Layout: Kim Henris; Cover Design: Jack Davis; Interior Art: Dorothy Hagstrom, David Gregory; Printer: Versa Press

Printed in the United States of America   10 9 8 7 6

Human Kinetics
P.O. Box 5076, Champaign, IL 61825-5076
1-800-747-4457

Canada: Human Kinetics, Box 24040, Windsor, ON N8Y 4Y9
1-800-465-7301 (in Canada only)

Europe: Human Kinetics, P.O. Box IW14, Leeds LS16 6TR, United Kingdom
(44) 1132 781708

Australia: Human Kinetics, 2 Ingrid Street, Clapham 5062, South Australia
(08) 371 3755

New Zealand: Human Kinetics, P.O. Box 105-231, Auckland 1
(09) 523 3462

Contents

Preface

Given our nearly 40 combined years of sports and games experiences, we are keenly aware of the need for a games book that not only reinforces the traditional sport skills emphasis in the middle school through high school years, but also provides a refreshing variety of challenging yet fun activities for our students. We recognized that the same old lead-up games and skill development drills, while useful to a point, often were devoid of the fun and enjoyment necessary for student enthusiasm and motivation.

We have been both professionals and volunteers in the world of games and sport—as secondary teachers and coaches; Little League assistants; community resource personnel; staff of varsity sports camps; members of curriculum study teams, advisory boards, and professional associations; and watchful parents. After long wishing for a book of games and skills activities to meet our needs, we finally took matters into our own hands.

Great Games for Young People meets the need for student fun and variety by offering nearly 70 games and skills activities to use on an impromptu basis or as a planned and integral part of the sport skill development process.

Each game is a self-contained and complete description with suggestions for modifications and variations to suit your situation. Each description outlines the game and its objectives, the number of players, the equipment and playing area that are needed, teaching strategies, and safety tips. Our objective is to help you involve children in active, meaningful, and safe learning situations emphasizing psychomotor skills, cognitive development, and affective social learning and cooperation. Each game has been tested to incorporate low organizational time, minimum or universal equipment, and adaptability to large-group instruction.

The games themselves encompass a wide range of interests and abilities, from problem solving in Human Checkers to lead-up skills for team sports, like in Blocker Soccer. Our handy Game Finder (pp. viii-xiii) lists all the games along with guidelines for ages and group sizes, gross motor ratings, and the types of skills involved.

We expect *Great Games for Young People* to appeal to all upper elementary, middle school, junior high, and senior high physical educators, as well as to YMCA directors, recreation therapists, camp directors, and youth sport coaches. Anyone who has faced the challenge of presenting meaningful activities to students when facilities suddenly change, numbers grow, or weather intervenes will find a wealth of ideas here. Or you may simply want to offer a fresh and fun change of pace during an ongoing unit of instruction. The application of these games is endless and can serve teachers and games leaders in a wide variety of situations. We hope you will find the book to be a useful resource.

Acknowledgments

We would like to thank our many colleagues for their ideas and our students for their enthusiasm in experimenting with the games. Our special thanks to Joel Determan, physical educator, for his contribution of games; to Matt Ellsworth, Anoka Hennepin District #11 physical education consultant–athletic coordinator, for his support and assistance during our project; and to Dot Hagstrom, friend and talented illustrator, for her valued assistance.

Guidelines for Safe and Effective Games

- Games should be suitable to student skills and ages and organized for maximum participation.
- The instructor should discuss safety precautions for each new game.
- Students should warm up and have a chance to practice new skills before each new game.
- Play environments should be free of obstacles and barriers.
- All games should be supervised by an instructor.
- The instructor should provide foam balls for games where students try to hit each other with balls.
- The value and enjoyment of any game rests on the teaching skills and enthusiasm of the instructor.

Game Finder

Use the Game Finder to identify games that are most appropriate for your group's age, size, skill level, and interest.

Basic skills

# Game	Grades	# per team	Gross motor rating	Throwing	Running	Kicking	Dodging	Shooting
1 Air Balloon	4-7	4-5	F					
2 Bases & Baskets	4-9	8-10	F	X	X			X
3 Bassoccet	7-12	10	G	X		X		X
4 Big Base	4-9	10-15	G	X	X			
5 Blind Buddy Relay	4-12	10	F					
6 The Blob Returns Relay	7-12	16-20	G		X			
7 Blocker Soccer	4-9	40-64	E		X	X		
8 Burn Ball	7-12	10-15	F	X	X			
9 Burn Rubber	7-12	10-15	E	X	X			
10 Cat & Mouse	4-12	10	G	X	X			
11 Catch a Thief	4-9	10	G		X			
12 Chocolate Roll	4-12	8-10	F					
13 Cleaning House	4-7	10-15	G	X				
14 Corner Catch	7-12	9	G	X				
15 Crazy Legs	4-9	10	G			X	X	
16 Dizzy Basketball Relay	4-12	3-4	F					
17 Double-Whammy Volleyball	7-12	6	E					
18 Ee-Tee Ball	7-12	10-15	E	X	X			
19 Escape From the OK Corral Relay	4-12	10	G		X			
20 Fire Ball	4-9	10	G	X				
21 Fistful	7-9	6	F					

Catching	Pushing	Dribbling	Problem solving	Stick handling	Soccer	Softball	Basketball	Volleyball	Hockey
								X	
							X		
			X						
					X				
X									
X									
	X								
X									
X									
X									
							X		
								X	
X									
X									
								X	

(Cont.)

Game Finder (Continued)

Basic skills

# Game	Grades	# per team	Gross motor rating	Throwing	Running	Kicking	Dodging	Shooting
22 Flickerball	7-12	6-40	E	X	X			
23 Four-Legged Soccer	7-12	8-12	E			X		
24 Frisbowl	4-9	8-12	F	X				
25 Funny Bone	4-12	10-15	G	X	X			X
26 Garbage Ball	7-12	12	G	X				X
27 Gate Tag	4-7	10-20	E		X		X	
28 Gotcha!	4-9	10-20	G		X			
29 Gusties	7-12	6-12	G	X				X
30 Hands Off!	7-12	10	G	X	X			
31 Hoosiers	7-12	10-15	F	X				
32 Human Checkers	7-12		NA					
33 Human Obstacle Relay	4-12	Any	E		X			
34 Indoor Snowball	9-12	10-15	G	X			X	
35 Lotsa Goalies	4-12	10-15	G					X
36 Mardi Gras	4-7	8-10	E		X		X	
37 Mission Impossible	4-12	10-15	F	X	X		X	
38 Move the Mountain	4-9	10	F	X				
39 The Number Scramble	4-7	10	F					
40 Pinball	4-9	Any	G	X			X	
41 Pinball Wizard	4-12	6-10	E	X				
42 222 Punt & Go	4-9	10	G	X	X			
43 Rat Ball	7-12	10-15	G	X	X			
44 Rat Tail Relay	4-12	8-10	G		X			
45 Rescue	4-12	Any	NA					

Sport skills

Catching	Pushing	Dribbling	Problem solving	Stick handling	Soccer	Softball	Basketball	Volleyball	Hockey
X									
		X							
X									
X									
		X							
X									
			X						
X									
				X					X
			X						
X									
X		X						X	
X							X		
X									
			X						

(Cont.)

Game Finder (Continued)

Basic skills

# Game	Grades	# per team	Gross motor rating	Throwing	Running	Kicking	Dodging	Shooting
46 Ruler of the Squares	4-9	4-8	F	X				
47 Run Like Crazy Relay	7-12	5-8	G	X	X			
48 Runners & Raggers	4-12	10-15	G					X
49 Secret Agent "007"	4-9	10	F	X	X		X	
50 Shoot-Out	7-12	10	F		X			X
51 Skink Ball	7-12	10-15	G		X	X		
52 Snow Rugby	9-12	10-40	E	X	X			
53 Speedy Sneakies	7-12	6-12	E	X				
54 Spider's Web	4-9	10	NA					
55 Square-Off Relay	4-12	6	G				X	
56 Stranded Relay	7-12	10	NA					
57 Sweepstakes	7-12	10-15	G		X			X
58 Team Toss	4-7	6	G	X				
59 Team Trivia	4-12	Any	NA					
60 Three-Pointer Relay	7-12	5-7	E					
61 Tic-Tac Volley	4-12	5-8	F					
62 Toss-Catch Basket Relay	7-12	4-6	F	X				
63 Triple Crown Baseball	4-12	10-15	G	X	X			
64 Volleyball Plus	7-12	6	E					
65 Volleysock	10-12	4-8	F					
66 Wheel of Torture	4-12	5-7	E		X			
67 When You're Hot You're Hot!	4-6	10-15	G		X			
68 Wolf's Den	4-12	6-12	F		X			
69 Zoney Ball	8-12	8-12	E					X

Sport skills

Catching	Pushing	Dribbling	Problem solving	Stick handling	Soccer	Softball	Basketball	Volleyball	Hockey
X									
X		X						X	
				X					X
X									
X									
			X						
			X						
				X					
X									
			X						
			X						
								X	
X									
X						X			
								X	
					X				
				X					X
							X		

1
AIR BALLOON

Objectives: Volleyball skills

Players: 4-5 per team

Equipment: 1 badminton net and standards for every 2 teams, 1 balloon for each court

Playing Area: Badminton courts

Gross Motor Activity Rating: Fair

Basic Skill Development Rating: Good

How to Play the Game: Divide the class into an even number of teams of 4 to 5 per team. Teams assume positions on a court as in volleyball. The object of the game is to score points using volleyball skills.

Play begins by any player tossing the balloon over the net to the opponents, who hit the balloon back using any type of hit. There is no limit on the number of hits a team may use. Holding and kicking are not allowed. The person serving always says the score. Both teams rotate clockwise after each point. Play is restarted immediately by the team with possession of the balloon, regardless of who scored the point.

One point is scored each time a team hits the balloon to the floor of their opponent's court. You don't need to be serving to score a point.

Play continues until a team scores 15 points or a time limit is reached.

Teaching Tips: Divide the players into teams of equal strength.

Variation: Use a heavy rubber balloon to speed the game up.

Variation: Divide each court into 2 courts, using floor tape as the net.

2
BASES & BASKETS

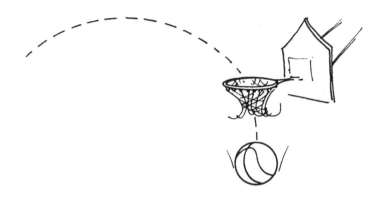

Objectives: Throwing, running, shooting, basketball skills

Players: 8-10 per team (2 teams)

Equipment: 1 basketball goal, 1 basketball, 4 cones

Playing Area: Gymnasium

Gross Motor Activity Rating: Fair

Basic Skill Development Rating: Fair

How to Play the Game: Teams assume batting and fielding positions as in softball; assign a number to each player on each team.

Number 1 on the batting team throws the ball from "home plate" as far into the field as possible and runs around the cones as if running bases.

Number 1 on the fielding team gets into shooting position near the goal. The fielding team must field the ball, passing it to each team member and to Number 1 last. Number 1 must then make a basket before the runner gets home; if not, a run is scored.

The remaining members of the batting team do selected calisthenics while their teammate is running the bases.

When batter Number 1 and fielder Number 1 are finished, the procedure is repeated for each number. Allow each player to bat in each inning.

The team with the most runs at the end of the game is the winner.

Teaching Tips: Divide the players into teams of equal strength.

You may vary the types of passes, the types of basketball shots, and the locomotor skills used.

For smaller children, use a volleyball or a foam ball.

Make sure the game ends with a completed inning.

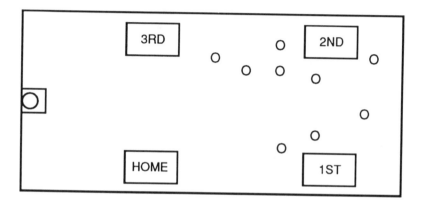

3
BASSOCCET

Objectives: Kicking, shooting, throwing

Players: 10 per team (2 teams)

Equipment: 2 basketball hoops, soccer ball (partially deflated)

Playing Area: Gymnasium

Gross Motor Activity Rating: Good

Basic Skill Development Rating: Good

How to Play the Game: Teams line up along their sidelines.

Five players from each team go onto the court for a jump ball to start the game. The remaining players on the sidelines are the goalies.

Player guidelines include the following:

- Unlimited passing is allowed among teammates on the sidelines or on the court.
- You cannot dribble the ball.
- A court player cannot pick the ball up off the floor, but can convert it by lifting it with the feet and then catching it.
- You can kick the ball to a teammate, who may catch it in the air.
- You can tap the ball to a goalie, who may pick it up and pass it to any teammate.
- Any player in the middle may take 3 steps before passing, shooting, throwing, or kicking the ball.

The court players remain in the middle for 1 to 3 minutes. When time is up, they go to the end of their lines and the next 5 go out.

4

The object of the game is to score points in the following ways (with only the 5 court players being able to score):

- By throwing the ball through the goalies and hitting the wall (1 point)
- By kicking the ball below shoulder level through the goalies and hitting the wall (3 points)
- By shooting the ball through your own basket (3 points)

If a basket is scored, the ball is immediately given to the end goalie on the opposite team.

Teaching Tips: Try to get equally skilled players in the middle at the same time. Rotate players between the court and sidelines often.

Safety Tips

Penalize players for unnecessary roughness, such as pushing or hitting.

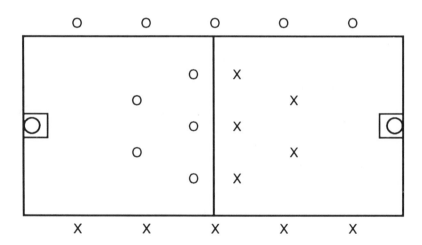

4
BIG BASE

Objectives: Running, throwing

Players: 10-15 per team (2 teams)

Equipment: 8'' foam ball, floor tape for bases and base path

Playing Area: Half or full gymnasium

Gross Motor Activity Rating: Good

Basic Skill Development Rating: Good

How to Play the Game: Divide the players into 2 equal teams. One team lines up at home plate, while the players on the other team space themselves randomly around the playing field.

To start the game, throw the ball to a corner of the gymnasium. Two runners take off toward second base. As soon as a runner is out or scores, another immediately starts to run, so that there are always 2 runners going. The runners must always stay to the right of the line (marked with floor tape) when running to second and back. The team in the field tries to get the runners out by hitting them with the ball below shoulder level.

The players in the field can take only 1 step with the ball; otherwise traveling is called. A runner cannot be put out by a fielder who travels. A player who travels may pass the ball to a teammate when traveling is called. All of the players on the batting team have 2 turns, and then the teams trade places.

The offense scores by players making it back to home plate safely, and the defense scores by tagging runners out. Play is continuous.

Teaching Tips: The best strategy for the defense is to keep the ball in front of the runners and pass to teammates in good positions to get runners out.

It is helpful to have several helpers count runs scored and call outs near second.

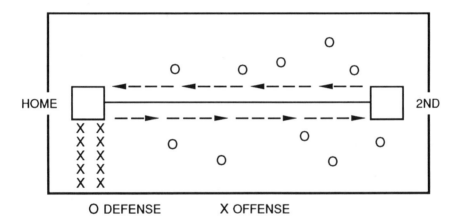

Safety Tips

It is an automatic run if a player throws at a runner in an unsafe manner.

HOME

2ND

O DEFENSE   X OFFENSE

5
BLIND BUDDY RELAY

Objectives: Vary, depending on the obstacles used

Players: 2 equal teams of about 10 per team

Equipment: 2 blindfolds, obstacles of your choice, floor tape to mark alleys

Playing Area: Gymnasium

Gross Motor Activity Rating: Fair

Basic Skill Development Rating: Good

How to Play the Game: Divide the class into 2 equal teams, with each team forming 2 lines as shown in the diagram. Teammates pair up, with 1 player blindfolded and the other being the guide.

The blind person must get through the racecourse listening to the directions given by the partner. The guide must not touch the blind person and must stay in the team's alley.

If any obstacles are knocked down, the blind person must fix that obstacle before continuing.

When the pair gets back to the start, the next pair begins. The team finishing first is the winner.

Teaching Tips: Move the obstacles periodically. Examples of obstacles include jumping rope 5 times, dribbling a basketball, crawling under a rope, stepping over a rope, and weaving around cones.

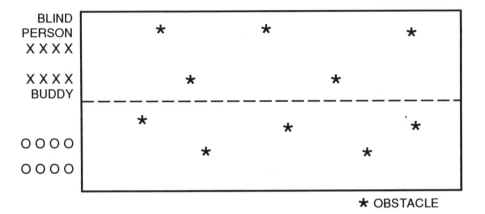

Safety Tips

Use obstacles requiring age-appropriate motor skills.

BLIND
PERSON
X X X X

X X X X
BUDDY

O O O O

O O O O

★ OBSTACLE

6
THE BLOB RETURNS RELAY

Objectives: Running

Players: Divide large group into teams of approximately 16-20

Equipment: Cones

Playing Area: Gymnasium

Gross Motor Activity Rating: Good

Basic Skill Development Rating: Good

How to Play the Game: On each team, all but 5 or 6 players form a "blob" by standing very close together; the remaining teammates circle around the group, facing away from the group and joining hands.

At the sound of the whistle, each group moves as one, down to the cone at the end of the gym, around it, and back.

The group that can stay intact and return to the starting line first wins.

Teaching Tips: This is a fun group effort. Remember to tell members of the blob that they may be traveling backward part of the time. Outside players can either hold hands or link elbows.

Safety Tips

It is a good idea to give the groups a slow practice session before the real race begins. This will eliminate surprises and familiarize players with their roles.

STARTING LINE

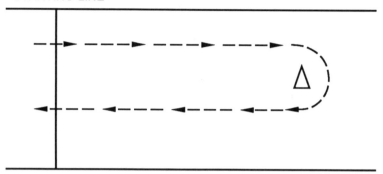

7
BLOCKER SOCCER

Objectives: Kicking, running, soccer skills

Players: 40-64 (2 teams)

Equipment: Soccer ball, pinnies to designate teams

Playing Area: Gymnasium

Gross Motor Activity Rating: Excellent

Basic Skill Development Rating: Excellent

How to Play the Game: Divide the group into 2 opposing teams. Then divide each team into 4 groups of 5 to 8 players. As indicated in the diagram, the 4 groups from each team are then placed in the following positions: Group 1 plays the game on court, Group 2 and Group 4 are positioned from the goal line to the centerline to defend the sidelines; Group 3 is positioned along the goal line to defend against the kicks made by the opposing team. Two players in Group 1 from each team play in Area A, and 2 players from each team play in Area C. These players may not leave their assigned areas. Two players from each team are placed in Area B and may cover the entire court.

The object of the game is to score goals as in soccer, using passing, kicking, and dribbling skills to advance the ball down the field.

The game begins with a kickoff by either team. When a goal has been scored, the team scored against kicks off from its defensive area (near corner). The game is played in 4- to 5-minute periods. Any time the ball goes between any of the goalies, is below waist height, and touches the back wall, 1 point is scored. The goals from all of the smaller groups count toward the total team scores.

At the end of each 5-minute period the groups rotate positions: 1 to 2 to 3 to 4 to 1.

The following infractions result in a free kick from the centerline: use of hands by a player (other than a goalie), unnecessary roughness, high kicking, or a sideline player permitting a ball to get through. Following an unsuccessful free kick, the ball is thrown in by a sideline player.

Teaching Tips: The game is best played as a lead-up to learning positioning and understanding the game of soccer. The key is to allow as many players as possible to have an active role. Provide for a quick transition to new positions.

Safety Tips

Keep players in their positions; this allows for free play with less chance of contact. Call free kicks for any unsportsmanlike conduct.

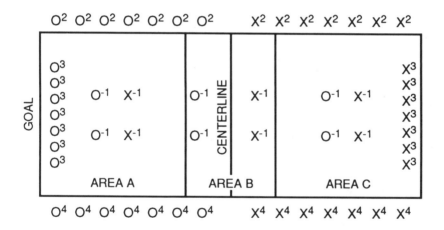

8
BURN BALL

Objectives: Running, throwing

Players: 10-15 per team (2 teams)

Equipment: 1 ball (volleyball, foam, or playground), floor tape for bases

Playing Area: Gymnasium

Gross Motor Activity Rating: Fair

Basic Skill Development Rating: Excellent

How to Play the Game: Divide the players into 2 equal teams. One team lines up at home plate, while the players on the other team space themselves randomly around the playing field. The fielding team must assign 1 player as the "burner."

The game begins with the first player throwing the ball into the field and running the bases. The fielding team fields the ball and gets it to the burner player, who must touch the ball to the "hot plate."

When the burner touches the ball to the hot plate, any runner who is not on a base is out and returns to the end of the throwing line.

Runners may stop at any base and stay there as long as they choose. Any number of runners may be on a base.

Runners who successfully run around all 4 bases score 1 point.

When a team has 3 outs, it becomes the fielding team.

Teaching Tips: If the teams are having difficulty making 3 outs, have them switch roles each time a team has gone through its batting order. Change the burner player often, because that person has the most ball contact.

Safety Tips

Give the batting team an automatic run if the fielders attempt to interfere with a runner.

O DEFENSE   X OFFENSE

9
BURN RUBBER

Objectives: Running, catching, throwing

Players: 10-15 per team (2 teams)

Equipment: 1 dense foam ball or whiffle ball, 4 bases, 1 tennis racquet

Playing Area: Gymnasium

Gross Motor Activity Rating: Excellent

Basic Skill Development Rating: Excellent

How to Play the Game: Divide the class into 2 teams, with 1 team up to bat and the other in the field.

The game starts with the first batter tossing the ball up and then hitting it with a small racquet or paddle, before the ball hits the floor. The player must pass the racquet to the next batter before proceeding to first base.

If the racquet touches the ground at any time after the hit and before the player reaches first base, the player is out.

Once on base, runners have the freedom to run or not to run.

There may be any number of players on any base at any time, running at their own paces, except that there must always be a batter—otherwise the inning is forfeited.

A player is out if

- the player swings and misses the ball 3 times,
- the outfield catches a fly ball,
- the player or a teammate drops the racquet or allows it to touch the floor, or
- a runner is tagged by the ball (held by a fielder, not thrown) while running to a base (there are no force outs).

There is no stealing or leading off. Runners may advance to another base once the ball is hit.

A run is scored each time a runner runs from 1st to 2nd to 3rd to 1st to 2nd to 3rd and then home (see diagram).

Teaching Tips: Rules may be adjusted to the class or the size of the playing area. Station the fielding team on bases and in the field as in softball.

> ## Safety Tips
> Do not allow the fielding players to stand too near the batter. Position them at a safe distance as in softball.

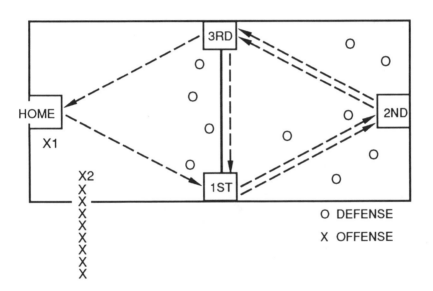

O DEFENSE

X OFFENSE

10
CAT & MOUSE

Objectives: Catching, running, throwing

Players: 10 per team (2 teams)

Equipment: A foam ball or Frisbee, 2 stopwatches, pinnies

Playing Area: Gymnasium

Gross Motor Activity Rating: Good

Basic Skill Development Rating: Excellent

How to Play the Game: The teams wear different colored pinnies. All players from both teams randomly spread out around the gym. The timekeeper holds 2 stopwatches, one for each team.

The game begins with the timekeeper throwing the ball (or Frisbee) into the air. As soon as a player takes possession of the ball, the timekeeper yells "Go!" and starts the watch for that team.

The player who gets the ball may either run with it or pass it to a teammate. All players are allowed anywhere on the field.

When the person with the ball is tagged by a member of the opposing team, the timekeeper stops the stopwatch and the player must immediately stop running and randomly toss the ball into the air. As soon as a player takes possession of the ball, the timekeeper again yells "Go!" and begins the watch for the team with possession.

The team that has kept possession of the ball for the longest amount of time is the winner.

Teaching Tips: It is helpful to have a timekeeper for each team.

Safety Tips

Penalize teams for unnecessary roughness, such as pushing or player contact other than tagging players.

11
CATCH A THIEF

Objectives: Running

Players: 10 per team (2 teams)

Equipment: 6 beanbags, floor tape to mark the jail

Playing Area: Gymnasium

Gross Motor Activity Rating: Good

Basic Skill Development Rating: Good

How to Play the Game: Divide the players into 2 equal teams, each team having half of the playing area. Place 3 beanbags on the back line of each side. Players try to capture the other team's beanbags. Players who carry one of the other team's beanbags back to their own side of the playing area without being tagged add that beanbag to their back line.

A player who is tagged on the opponents' side must go to jail. A teammate may rescue a prisoner by going into the jail, taking the prisoner's hand, and running the prisoner back to their side of the playing area. If rescuer and prisoner are tagged, they both become prisoners. Only 1 prisoner may be rescued at a time.

The first team to capture all of the opponents' beanbags wins.

Teaching Tips: The larger the playing area or the fewer the players, the more active the game will be. This game works well outside on a football field.

Ⓓ BEANBAGS

12
CHOCOLATE ROLL

Objectives: Pushing

Players: 8-10 per team (2 teams)

Equipment: Cageball or tied, rolled mat

Playing Area: Gymnasium

Gross Motor Activity Rating: Fair

Basic Skill Development Rating: Good

How to Play the Game: The teams should be equal distances from the mat or cageball, which is in the center of the gym.

On the "Go!" signal, the teams rush to the mat or ball and try to push it over the opposite end line.

One point is scored each time a team rolls the mat or ball over the end line.

Teaching Tips: For larger teams it is best to use a mat rather than a cageball.

Safety Tips

No unnecessary roughness is allowed. Do not have the teams begin too far away from the center mat.

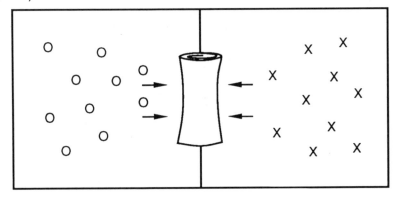

13
CLEANING HOUSE

Objectives: Catching, throwing

Players: 10-15 per team (2 teams)

Equipment: Any odd number of foam or soft playground balls (9 or more is suggested), volleyball net and standards

Playing Area: Gymnasium

Gross Motor Activity Rating: Good

Basic Skill Development Rating: Excellent

How to Play the Game: Divide the players into 2 equal teams. The players on each team randomly spread out on their sides of the net. As evenly as possible, divide the balls between the 2 sides.

The object is for each team to keep throwing balls over the net to the opponents' side so that when the time limit has expired there will be as many balls as possible in the other team's possession.

The time limit is unknown to the players so that they do not hoard the balls and throw them over at the last possible moment.

A game is played in quarters of 1 to 3 minutes each. Four quarters constitute a game. At the end of each quarter the balls on each side of the net are counted. The totals from all 4 quarters are added together, and the team with the lowest number wins the game.

Teaching Tips: Make sure that the balls are never held for more than a couple of seconds, to insure maximum participation. Teams should take turns receiving the greater number of balls at the beginning of a quarter.

Safety Tips

Penalize the team of any player who throws the ball over the net in a harmful manner.

14
CORNER CATCH

Objectives: Catching, throwing

Players: 9 per team (2 teams)

Equipment: Basketball or volleyball, floor tape to mark goal area (approximately 3' × 3')

Playing Area: Gymnasium or playground, size of a basketball court

Gross Motor Activity Rating: Good

Basic Skill Development Rating: Good

How to Play the Game: The teams have equal numbers of players, consisting of ''guards'' and two goalies. Two players from each team position themselves in the corners of their opponents' territory.

The object of the game is for a guard to throw the ball over the heads of the opposing guards (see diagram) to one of the goalies in the corner goal. A point is earned for each successful pass. The goalie must catch the ball in the air.

The ball is tossed in the center to start the game, and a point is made each time a corner goalie catches the ball while both feet are in the goal area. Play is continuous. When a goalie receives the ball, she or he immediately throws it back to one of the guards. A guard may pass the ball to another guard or directly to one of the goalies. An out-of-bounds ball is recovered and put into play by the opposite team, near the point where it went out. The game is played in 3- to 5-minute time shifts, with replacement players coming in during each shift change.

It is a foul for a guard to step across the centerline. The ball is given to the nearest opponent when a foul is committed. The team with the most points wins!

Teaching Tips: As a lead-up skill game to basketball, basketball rules—such as those for traveling, dribbling, and passing—may be used. The game can be played with free movement, carrying and passing at will. The game is best played with some restrictions on ball-carrying so that no one player dominates.

Safety Tips

There is no contact between players, but instruct players to watch the ball at all times to avoid getting hit by the ball. A foam ball may be substituted, for smaller players.

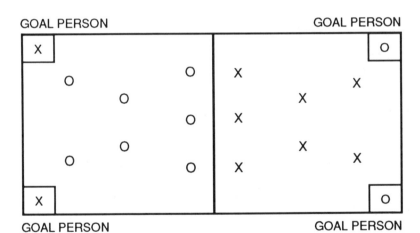

15
CRAZY LEGS

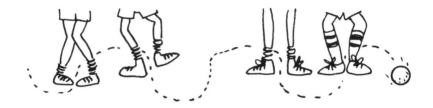

Objectives: Catching, kicking, running

Players: 10 per team (2 teams)

Equipment: 1 ball (soccer, volleyball, playground, or foam)

Playing Area: Gymnasium

Gross Motor Activity Rating: Good

Basic Skill Development Rating: Good

How to Play the Game: Divide the class into 2 equal teams. One team lines up, and the players on the other team space themselves randomly around the playing field.

The game begins with the pitcher rolling the ball to the kicker, who kicks the ball into the field. (A player on the fielding team fields the ball, and all the teammates line up behind the person with the ball. The front person in the line must roll the ball back between the legs of the teammates. When the last person in line gets the ball, that player holds it in the air. The kicker, meanwhile, tries to run around the bases before the fielding team accomplishes all this.

If the kicker gets home first, he or she scores a point. If the fielders finish first, they score a point. The kickers become the fielders once everyone on the team has kicked.

Teaching Tips: The number of bases or the distance between bases may be changed according to skill level or number of players involved. Adjustments may be made after the first innings.

Safety Tips

Penalize teams for unnecessary roughness, such as interfering with a runner.

16
DIZZY BASKETBALL RELAY

Objectives: Basketball skills, relay

Players: 3-4 per team (4 teams)

Equipment: 4 basketballs, 4 cones

Playing Area: Basketball court

Gross Motor Activity Rating: Fair

Basic Skill Development Rating: Good

How to Play the Game: Divide the class into 4 equal teams and line them up on the sidelines of the basketball court as shown in the diagram.

Each basketball is placed on a cone in the center of the gym. Any team is allowed to use any basketball.

On the whistle the first person for each team runs out, places a hand on a ball, and runs around the cone 1 to 3 times (as determined by you). The player then dribbles to either basket and must make 1 basket before running back and putting the ball on an empty cone. The player then runs and touches the next player in line, who does the same.

The first team to finish is the winner.

Teaching Tips: If you have more than 3 or 4 per team, divide the class into 8 teams with 4 teams playing on each half of the gym. In this case each group of 4 teams will be shooting at 1 basket only.

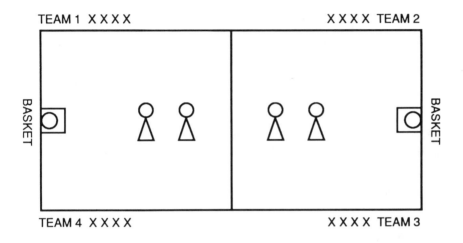

TEAM 1 X X X X   X X X X TEAM 2

BASKET   BASKET

TEAM 4 X X X X   X X X X TEAM 3

17
DOUBLE-WHAMMY VOLLEYBALL

Objectives: Volleyball skills

Players: 4 teams of 6 players each

Equipment: 3 standards, 2 volleyball nets, 2 volleyballs of different colors (spray paint one)

Playing Area: 2 volleyball courts side by side

Gross Motor Activity Rating: Excellent

Basic Skill Development Rating: Excellent

How to Play the Game: Each team of 6 sets up as for regulation volleyball.

Both balls are put into play with a regulation volleyball serve to the team directly across the net. The same color ball is always served on the same court. Example: The blue ball is always served on Court 1.

Immediately following the serve, the 2 teams on the same side of the net play as 1 large team (A vs. B), and the boundaries are extended to form 1 large court. Either ball can be played on either court, but the players must remain on their own courts at all times.

During the volleys, regulation volleyball rules apply. When 1 ball is dead, play continues with the remaining ball until it is also dead. Once both balls are dead, players rotate and the 2 balls are served at the same time.

Scoring is the same as in volleyball. Each subteam keeps its own score (only scoring when serving). The game ends when 1 of the 4 teams scores 15 points. The scores are then added together (A-1 and A-2, and B-1 and B-2), and the team with the highest number wins.

Teaching Tips: Divide the teams into players of equal strength. For younger or less skilled players you may want to use a foam volleyball.

Safety Tips

Do not allow any uncontrolled or rough play. Officiate
the game. Encourage players to play their positions on
the court to avoid collisions.

X			X	X			X
	X				X		
X	A-1		X	X	A-2		X
	X				X		

NET

	O				O		
O	B-1		O	O	B-2		O
	O				O		
O			O	O			O

COURT 1   COURT 2

18
EE-TEE BALL

Objectives: Catching, running, throwing

Players: 10-15 per team (2 teams)

Equipment: 2 portable goals, 1 Frisbee

Playing Area: Gymnasium

Gross Motor Activity Rating: Excellent

Basic Skill Development Rating: Good

How to Play the Game: Divide the players into 2 equal teams. Each team has 1 player in the goal and the remaining players on their half of the playing area as shown in the diagram.

The Frisbee is put into play by a designated player throwing it into the air anywhere on the court. Once the Frisbee has been thrown, players may move anywhere on the playing area.

The player who catches the Frisbee runs toward the opponents' goal until she or he is tagged. Once tagged, the player must stop and release the Frisbee by throwing or dropping within 3 seconds; otherwise the other team gains possession.

If 2 players grab the Frisbee at the same time, a "jump saucer" (the same as a jump ball in basketball) is called.

A throw at the goal may be made from anywhere except within the penalty area. The goalie is the only player allowed in the penalty area and may leave and enter at any time.

One point is scored each time the Frisbee goes into the goal net.

Teaching Tips: Divide the players into teams of equal strength. The game is more successful if the teams remain spread out over the playing area by playing positions as in soccer.

Safety Tips

Penalize teams for unnecessary roughness, such as pushing or tackling.

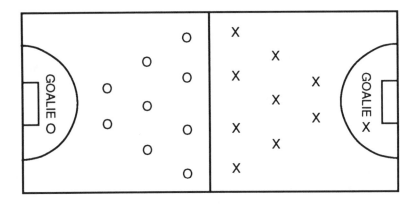

19
ESCAPE FROM THE OK CORRAL RELAY

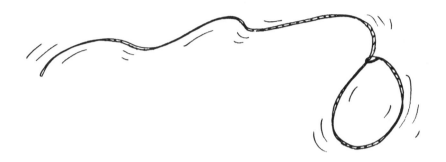

Objectives: Running

Players: 10 per team

Equipment: 25- to 30-foot rope for each team

Playing Area: Gymnasium

Gross Motor Activity Rating: Good

Basic Skill Development Rating: Fair

How to Play the Game: Divide the class into equal teams of about 10 per team. Each team has a rope tied around the entire team at waist height.

On the whistle each team races down to and around its cone and back across the finish line.

Teaching Tips: Divide the players into teams of equal strength.

Safety Tips

The teams should be instructed to move at speeds that enable the slower students to keep up.

Make sure that the students are not pressed tightly against each other by having the rope too tight. Students are allowed to hold the rope up if necessary.

20
FIRE BALL

Objectives: Catching, throwing

Players: 10 per team (2 teams)

Equipment: Pinnies, 1 ball (basketball, volleyball, or foam)

Playing Area: Gymnasium

Gross Motor Activity Rating: Good

Basic Skill Development Rating: Good

How to Play the Game: Players spread out randomly over the playing area. The object of the game is to use passing and catching skills to keep the ball away from the opponents.

Start the game by randomly throwing the ball into the playing area. The player with the ball may not move with the ball and must pass it within 3 seconds. Other players may move anywhere in the playing area. The defensive team may intercept passes and knock the ball away but must not contact the player with the ball.

The score is determined by the number of completed passes made in succession by 1 team.

Teaching Tips: Players can shout out the number of completed passes to add to the excitement.

If certain players seem to dominate the game, make a rule that players may not pass the ball back to the players they receive the ball from. You may also require the passes to alternate boy–girl.

Safety Tips

Penalize teams for unnecessary roughness, such as pushing or hitting.

21
FISTFUL

Objectives: Volleyball skills

Players: 6 per team

Equipment: Lightweight or foam ball (volleyball size or smaller), volleyball net 6' high

Playing Area: Volleyball court

Gross Motor Activity Rating: Fair

Basic Skill Development Rating: Excellent

How to Play the Game: Each team has 6 players on the court: 3 in the forward line and 3 in the back line, deep in the court.

The game begins when the ball is put in play by a toss from a forward. The back-line player directly behind moves forward and bats the ball with a closed fist. The ball may be hit in any direction with a closed fist or with the inside of the forearm in a forehand motion. Fundamental movement is under and up to pass the ball to a teammate, and overhead and downward to send the ball to the opponents' court. The ball is not dead until it has bounced twice on the floor without being contacted.

A player may hit the ball only once in a row; then the ball must be played by another player before the first player may hit it again. In a small gym the ball may be played off the wall. After each 5 points scored by a side, players switch from forward to back-line positions. Serve is given to the side that has possession of the ball.

A team scores a point when the ball bounces twice on the floor on the opponents' side. Play to 20 points.

Teaching Tips: If players are ready to progress, add a 2-handed bump pass.

Safety Tips

Be ready to substitute a smaller ball if the large one seems too difficult to control or players shy away from it.

Be sure to emphasize to the players that their fists must remain closed.

22
FLICKERBALL

Objectives: Running, catching, throwing

Players: 6-40 (2 teams)

Equipment: Foam football, 4 cones, pinnies or vests for half of group

Playing Area: Gymnasium

Gross Motor Activity Rating: Excellent

Basic Skill Development Rating: Excellent

How to Play the Game: Divide players into 2 equal teams. Players scatter about the gymnasium. Each player stands near an opponent in a person-to-person defense.

Start the game by having 1 team take the ball at their own 10-yard line. The football may be advanced only by passing and catching. A player must stop immediately after receiving a pass and then pass the ball within 5 seconds. The opponents cannot defend the passer; they must remain 5 yards from the passer, and if the ball touches the floor, it immediately goes to the possession of the other team. There are an unlimited number of downs, as the ball is continuously in play.

It is a touchdown when a player catches a pass in the end zone. All touchdowns are worth 1 point. After a point is scored, the nonscoring team begins play by throwing the ball from their own 10-yard line.

Teaching Tips: The game is played best when the offensive team spreads out and keeps moving while the defensive team plays person-to-person defense.

Safety Tips

Penalize teams for unnecessary roughness, such as guarding too closely. The game is played best when players are not too crowded.

The game is fast-moving, so players could rotate in shifts of teams if play seems too congested.

23
FOUR-LEGGED SOCCER

Objectives: Kicking

Players: 8-12 per team (2 teams)

Equipment: Cageball

Playing Area: Small gymnasium

Gross Motor Activity Rating: Excellent

Basic Skill Development Rating: Good

How to Play the Game: Each team divides its players into an offensive line, a defensive line, and 1 goalie, as shown in the diagram. All players take the crab position (body supine, movement forward and back supported by both feet and both hands).

Start the game by rolling the ball down the centerline to the middle of the front-row players.

All players must play their positions and move together within their lines. The defensive team must not move in front of their own team's offensive line during play.

Only the goalies may use their hands to stop the ball.

One point is scored each time a team kicks the ball and it hits the opponents' wall.

Teaching Tips: After a point is scored, have the lines rotate from offense to defense and rotate the goalie. Because this game is physically very tiring, rotate in any substitutes often.

Safety Tips

Penalize teams for unnecessary roughness, such as kicking any player.

```
                              X
                    X                    X           O
GOALIE X    X    DEFENSIVE LINE    X    OFFENSIVE LINE    OFFENSIVE LINE  O    DEFENSIVE LINE  O    GOALIE O
            X                     X                       O                              O
            X                     X                       O                              O
                                  X                       O
```

24
FRISBOWL

Objectives: Throwing

Players: 8-12 per team (2 teams)

Equipment: 20 or more plastic bowling pins, and 6 Frisbees, 3 each of 2 colors

Playing Area: Half of a basketball court

Gross Motor Activity Rating: Fair

Basic Skill Development Rating: Good

How to Play the Game: Divide the class into 2 teams with each team forming 3 lines behind the end line, as shown in the diagram.

Each front-row player has a Frisbee (for example: 3 blue Frisbees for the O team and 3 red Frisbees for the X team).

On the whistle, all 6 players throw their Frisbees at the pins on their sides of the court. The first person in line A quickly retrieves his or her team's 3 Frisbees and hands them to the next 3 people, who immediately throw at the remaining pins. This continues until 1 team has knocked down all the pins.

Teaching Tips: After each game, set the pins up in a different pattern.

Instead of only 1 person retrieving all 3 Frisbees, you may have all throwers retrieve their own.

Safety Tips

If all throwers retrieve their own Frisbees, make the
rule that the team must wait for all 3 Frisbees to be
returned before the next 3 may be thrown. This will
prevent the retrievers from being hit with Frisbees.

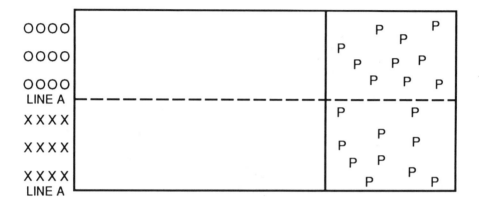

25
FUNNY BONE

Objectives: Running, shooting, throwing

Players: 10-15 per team (2 teams)

Equipment: 1 ball, floor tape for bases, 1 basket

Playing Area: Gymnasium

Gross Motor Activity Rating: Good

Basic Skill Development Rating: Good

How to Play the Game: One team lines up behind home plate while the other team assigns 1 player to each base and scatters the remaining players throughout the playing area.

The game begins with the first player in the batting line serving the ball underhand (as in volleyball) far into the field. That person then runs to touch the target on the opposite wall and returns to home plate before the fielding team makes a basket.

To make an out the fielding team must field the ball, throw it to first, second, and third bases, and then make a basket before the runner gets home.

The teams switch after 3 outs or 1 time through the batting order.

Each successful run scores 1 point.

Teaching Tips: You may want to rotate the players on base with those scattered in the field after each served ball to assure more participation by each player.

Also you may require that a different player shoot the basket each time.

If the runners are consistently beating the fielding team, you may need to alter the running path by making the batter run twice or dribble a basketball while running.

Safety Tips

Penalize the fielding team if they interfere with the runner. When the ball is being served, have all the fielders stand behind an imaginary line running from first to third base.

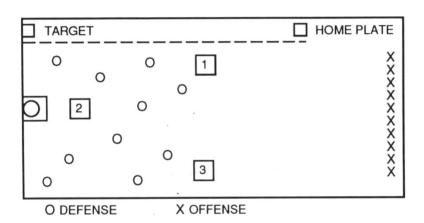

O DEFENSE   X OFFENSE

26
GARBAGE BALL

Objectives: Dribbling, shooting, throwing

Players: 12 per team (2 teams)

Equipment: 2 large wastepaper baskets, 1 ball (playground or basketball), floor tape, pinnies

Playing Area: Gymnasium

Gross Motor Activity Rating: Good

Basic Skill Development Rating: Excellent

How to Play the Game: Divide the players into 2 equal teams with 5 from each team playing on the court and 1 goalie per team. The remaining players are spread out along the sidelines as shown in the diagram.

An area approximately 10 feet from the wall and 10 feet across is taped at both ends of the playing field.

The game is similar to basketball, with the following changes. Scoring is done by shooting the ball into a wastepaper basket held by the goalie, who is standing in a 2-foot taped square. The goalie may move the basket to help catch the ball but must not step out of the square.

The players on the sides must stay behind the sidelines but may receive passes from the on-court players.

No player is allowed inside the 10-foot area, so all shots at the basket must be outside the 10-foot taped area.

Rotate the court and sideline players every 3 to 5 minutes.

Jump balls, fouls, and scoring are the same as in basketball.

Teaching Tips: Divide the players into teams of equal strength. For younger children you may want to use a foam ball.

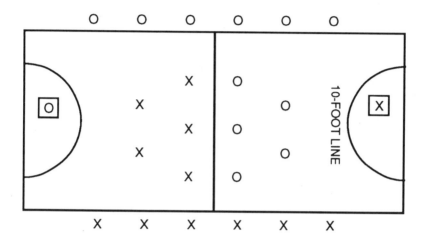

27
GATOR TAG

Objectives: Dodging, running

Players: 10-20

Equipment: 1 rope approximately 20' long

Playing Area: Gymnasium or playground with boundaries

Gross Motor Activity Rating: Excellent

Basic Skill Development Rating: Fair

How to Play the Game: All players are randomly scattered throughout the gymnasium with 1 person being the gator.

The gator pulls around a rope and tries to tag the other players. Tagged players must join the gator by hanging on to the rope.

Play continues until the gator has all the players on the rope.

Teaching Tips: This is a good cardiovascular exercise and may be used as a warm-up to other activities. Or, as each new gator is selected for a turn, you might keep track of the time it takes for each gator to collect all players. The top gator would be the fastest.

Safety Tips

Penalize any player on the gator rope who tries to restrict the gator in any way.

28
GOTCHA!

Objectives: Catching, running

Players: Two teams of 10-20 per team

Equipment: 6 bases, small foam ball, tennis racquet or large paddle

Playing Area: Gymnasium

Gross Motor Activity Rating: Good

Basic Skill Development Rating: Good

How to Play the Game: The 2 teams have equal numbers of players. The team in the field has 6 people on base with the remainder scattered about the field of play.

The runner begins by hitting the ball and running to first base. When a ball is hit, all base runners must run at least 1 base but may run more if they choose. When a runner gets to sixth base, a point is scored.

The fielders put the runners out by fielding the ball and throwing it to a catcher on any base, who shouts "Gotcha!" as soon as she or he catches the ball. Any runner who is not safely on a base when "Gotcha!" is called would be out. When there are 3 outs, the fielding and hitting teams switch roles.

Any number of players may be on a base at once, as long as there is still a team member available to bat. If no one is left to bat, the batting team becomes the fielding team.

The team with the most points at the end of the game is the winner.

Teaching Tips: Several "spotters" can assist on calls to determine whether the runners are safe or out.

Rather than switching sides after 3 outs, teams could go through the entire lineup, counting the number of runs in for the team and then switching.

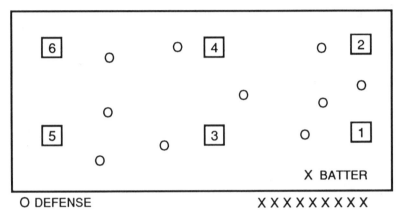

O DEFENSE

X OFFENSE

29
GUSTIES

Objectives: Catching, shooting, throwing

Players: 6-12 per team (2 teams)

Equipment: 1 ball (foam, partially deflated volleyball, or playground), 2 baskets

Playing Area: Gymnasium basketball court

Gross Motor Activity Rating: Good

Basic Skill Development Rating: Good

How to Play the Game: The 2 teams have equal numbers of players on the court, and 2 players each in the end zones. If the game is played with fewer people, 1 player in each end zone is fine.

The game begins with a jump ball. Players may not hold the ball longer than 2 seconds. A player may take no more than 2 steps and may not dribble the ball. The referee awards the ball to the opponents on a rule violation.

Players may not touch the ball while it is in the opponents' hands. All areas are considered in-bounds. The ball may be bounced off the wall and caught to advance the play or score in the end zone. After a goal, the team not scoring starts play with a throw-in from its end zone.

Throwing the ball to a teammate who is in the end zone scores 1 point, and shooting a basket counts 2 points.

Teaching Tips: You might have the players take responsibility for guarding an area or zone of play, or guarding a specific player when in a defensive strategy.

Safety Tips

Penalize teams for unnecessary roughness. General rules of basketball can be followed to keep this a non-contact sport.

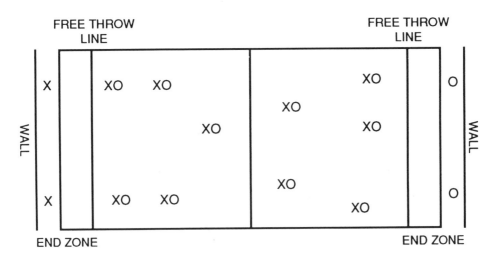

30
HANDS OFF!

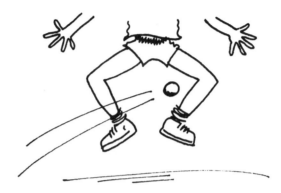

Objectives: Throwing, dribbling, running

Players: 10 per team (4 teams)

Equipment: 4 portable soccer goals, 2 foam balls

Playing Area: Gymnasium

Gross Motor Activity Rating: Good

Basic Skill Development Rating: Good

How to Play the Game: Divide the playing area in half and make two courts as shown in the diagram.

Each team has 6 players on the court and 4 players on the sidelines as shown in the diagram. One player on each team acts as goalkeeper.

The object of the game is to use dribbling and passing skills to advance the ball down the court to score a goal.

The game begins with a jump ball. Players may move anywhere on the court. However, players with the ball can take only 2 steps and dribble only twice. No player may hold the ball for more than 5 seconds. Players on the sidelines may receive passes and score goals, but they cannot cross the restraining line in doing so.

To score, a player must throw the ball into the goal net. Each goal is worth 1 point.

Teaching Tips: If a few players appear to dominate the game, institute a rule that there must be a certain number of passes before a goal can be attempted. If sideline players are left out of the action, use a similar rule saying that every other pass must be to the sideline. Rotate players between the court and the sideline often.

Safety Tips

Penalize teams for unnecessary roughness, such as pushing or hitting.

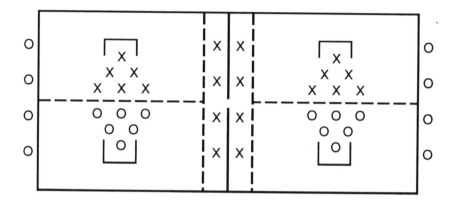

31
HOOSIERS

Objectives: Catching, throwing

Players: 10-15 per team (2 teams)

Equipment: Floor tape for bases, 1 ball

Playing Area: Gymnasium

Gross Motor Activity Rating: Fair

Basic Skill Development Rating: Good

How to Play the Game: Each team assigns 5 players to play on the bases (4 forwards and 1 captain), and the remaining players are scattered across the field as shown in the diagram.

The game begins with a jump ball at center court. The guards attempt to throw the ball to their forwards, who are the only players who can throw the ball to the captain.

Captains and forwards are allowed to have 1 foot off the base but never 2. No guard can run with the ball or hold it longer than 3 seconds.

One point is scored every time the captain gets the ball. After a point is made, the nonscoring team takes possession anywhere in the backcourt.

Teaching Tips: Divide the players into teams of equal strength. You may require the guards to make a certain number of passes among themselves before passing to the forwards. Rotate the guards, captains, and forwards often.

Safety Tips

No player contact or unnecessary roughness is allowed.

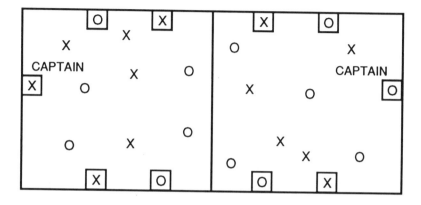

32
HUMAN CHECKERS

Objectives: Problem solving

Players: For each checker game, use 1 player less than the number of squares marked on the floor. Several teams play at the same time.

Equipment: Floor tape to mark small squares (1') on the floor.

Playing Area: Small portion of gymnasium

Gross Motor Activity Rating: NA

Basic Skill Development Rating: NA

How to Play the Game: Each team has 1 player on each of the squares, except that the center square is left open.

The object of the game is for the X and O players to exchange places by moving 1 person at a time around each other.

The first play would be for 1 player to move to the open square. No player can "jump" a teammate or move backward on the floor.

The first team to complete the move to the opposite side is the winner.

Teaching Tips: Instruct players to step only in the squares, to prevent getting mixed up. The game appears easier than it actually is. Remember, only 1 player moves at a time, as in real checkers.

Safety Tips

No pushing is allowed.

GAME 1
(6 STUDENTS)

| O |
| O |
| O |
| ☐ |
| X |
| X |
| X |

GAME 2
(6 STUDENTS)

| O |
| O |
| O |
| ☐ |
| X |
| X |
| X |

33
HUMAN OBSTACLE RELAY

Objectives: Running, varying with the obstacles used

Players: Any number, divided into 2 or more equal teams

Equipment: None

Playing Area: Gymnasium or outdoor play area

Gross Motor Activity Rating: Excellent

Basic Skill Development Rating: Fair

How to Play the Game: Players are divided into equal groups of 8 to 16 per team. Two or more teams are needed.

The object of the relay is to use gross motor activity in a relay of obstacles provided by teammates. No equipment is used; members of each team become obstacles for their own team. All teams have the same obstacles. For example, Obstacle 1 is to circle twice around a standing player, Obstacle 2 is to jump as high as possible to reach a "high-5" hand clap with a "tall" obstacle player, and Obstacle 3 is to run around several human obstacles in a slalom pattern (or figure 8). You can ask players to slide, jump, or even move backward. After the first player completes the obstacle course, that player becomes the last obstacle and all other obstacle players move up 1 position. The first obstacle player goes to the end of the appropriate relay line.

Teaching Tips: It is your responsibility to make the activity appropriate for coed situations. The obstacles must not put players in awkward or embarrassing positions.

Allow players to create some of their own obstacles; this adds problem-solving activity and interest to the relay.

> ## Safety Tips
>
> No obstacles should put players in positions where they might get pushed, stepped on, or hurt in any way. Evaluate obstacles before each relay begins.

34
INDOOR SNOWBALL

Objectives: Catching, dodging, throwing

Players: 10-15 per team (2 teams)

Equipment: Floor tape to mark war zone and prisons, 10-15 foam balls

Playing Area: Gymnasium

Gross Motor Activity Rating: Good

Basic Skill Development Rating: Excellent

How to Play the Game: Each team is spread out over its half of the gym as shown in the diagram.

The object of the game is to capture all opponents.

Any player from either team may enter the neutral zone in the center.

When a player is hit by a fly ball below the shoulders, that person goes to prison using the trail as shown in the diagram. Prisoners all escape if a teammate throws the "bomb-ball" into the prison and a prisoner catches the ball on the fly. Designate which ball is to be the "bomb" by its size or color. It must be different from the other balls used.

When prisoners leave the prison, make sure they use the trail out to avoid collisions with players entering prison.

When all the members of a team are in prison, the other team is declared the winner.

Teaching Tips: If the boys appear to be dominating the game, institute a rule that every 30 to 45 seconds only girls may throw and the next 30 to 45 seconds only boys may throw.

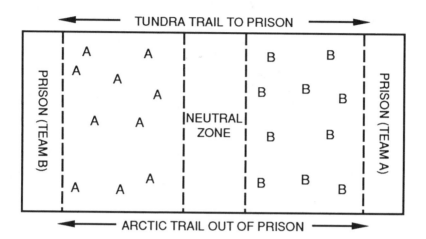

35
LOTSA GOALIES

Objectives: Shooting, stickhandling, hockey skills

Players: 10-15 per team (2 teams)

Equipment: Hockey sticks, tennis ball

Playing Area: Gymnasium

Gross Motor Activity Rating: Good

Basic Skill Development Rating: Excellent

How to Play the Game: Each team assigns 3 players as forwards and 3 as halfbacks. The remaining players become goalies in the end zone as shown in the diagram.

The game begins with a face-off at center court. Each center forward touches the ground, then touches sticks with the opponent 3 times. Following this, each tries to play the ball until one succeeds. Play continues by passing the ball until 1 team scores a goal.

The goalies are not allowed to leave the end-zone area.

After each goal, or after 5 minutes of play, rotate players in the court and goalie positions.

Penalty shots are given for high sticking or body contact. A penalty shot is a free shot taken from the penalty mark by any player.

The goal area should be marked with a tape line running across the end-zone area at about shoulder height of the players. One point is scored by the team that hits the ball against the wall below the tape.

Teaching Tips: Explain positions to the players so they understand what areas the forwards and halfbacks are responsible for.

For younger students a tennis ball may move too fast, and you may want to try a small foam ball or a foam puck.

Safety Tips

Make sure the players are playing their positions and are not bunching around the ball.

Penalize players for unnecessary roughness.

END ZONE

```
X  |  HALFBACKS                                    |  O
X  |     X     X              O     O              |  O
X  |                                               |  O
   |   * X     X              O     O *            |
X  |                                               |  O
   |     X     X              O     O              |  O
X  |       FORWARDS                                |
X  |                                               |  O
```

*PENALTY MARK

36
MARDI GRAS

Objectives: Running, dodging

Players: 8-10 in a group, with as many groups as space allows

Equipment: 1 flag-football belt per group

Playing Area: Gymnasium

Gross Motor Activity Rating: Excellent

Basic Skill Development Rating: Good

How to Play the Game: Each group forms a line, with the players putting their arms around the waists of the players in front of them. The last person in the line puts on the flag-football belt.

The object of the game is to capture the ''tail'' (flag) of another group before the whistle blows signifying the end of the round. A point is given for each flag captured. When the round ends, the person at the head of the line goes to the end and wears the belt, and everyone else advances 1 position.

Each round goes 3 minutes. Each group must be moving during the round.

Teaching Tips: This is a great warm-up activity for large groups. After several rounds everyone is actively involved and ready to move on to more fun. Perhaps the group collecting the most belts can be rewarded by choosing the game or activity to be enjoyed next!

Safety Tips

No unnecessary roughness or pushing is allowed. Players cannot touch players in other groups.

37
MISSION IMPOSSIBLE

Objectives: Dodging, running, throwing

Players: 10-15 per team (2 teams)

Equipment: Floor tape for bases, foam ball

Playing Area: Gymnasium

Gross Motor Activity Rating: Fair

Basic Skill Development Rating: Good

How to Play the Game: One team lines up behind home plate, and the other is scattered randomly in the field.

The game is started by the leadoff player throwing the ball as hard as possible into the field. The leadoff player and the next player in line begin running to the base and back to home. As soon as a runner either is out or scores a point, the next player in line begins running, so there are always 2 runners. There is no stopping on base.

The batting team runs once through its lineup and then switches with the fielders. The batting team is allowed only the 1 throw that starts the inning.

The team in the field attempts to get the runners out by hitting them with the ball below the shoulders. The fielders are not allowed to take any steps once they pick up the ball.

The batting team scores 1 point for every runner who makes it home without being hit.

Teaching Tips: It is helpful to shout ''Go!'' as soon as a new runner should begin, to keep the game moving quickly.

Safety Tips

Penalize any player for interfering with a runner or throwing the ball at the runners in a harmful manner.

38
MOVE THE MOUNTAIN

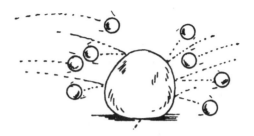

Objectives: Throwing

Players: 10 per team (2 teams)

Equipment: 1 large cageball, 20 balls (playground, foam, or volleyballs)

Playing Area: Gymnasium

Gross Motor Activity Rating: Fair

Basic Skill Development Rating: Excellent

How to Play the Game: Each team lines up behind its restraining line with half of the balls. The object of the game is to move the cageball by hitting it with the thrown balls.

Players may leave the restraining areas to retrieve balls on their halves of the gym, but they must return to the restraining areas to throw.

When a team moves the ball across the goal line, it scores 1 point.

Teaching Tips: If the boys appear to be dominating the throwing, institute a rule that for 30 to 45 seconds only girls may throw and for the next 30 to 45 seconds only the boys may throw. The next 30 to 45 seconds you may want everyone to throw.

Safety Tips

Penalize the team of any player who throws a ball at an opposing player.

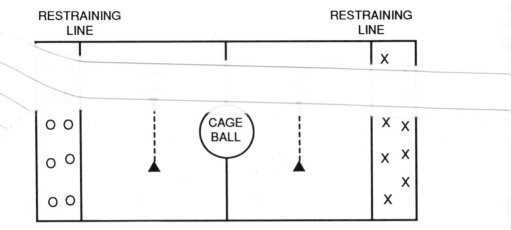

39
THE NUMBER SCRAMBLE

Objectives: Problem solving

Players: 10 per team

Equipment: None

Playing Area: Gymnasium

Gross Motor Activity Rating: Fair

Basic Skill Development Rating: Fair

How to Play the Game: Divide the players into teams of about ten. Position yourself high enough above the players that you can see them all.

Call out a number. The players on each team assemble themselves to form that number.

The first team to most accurately form the number scores 1 point. The team with the most points at the end of the playing time is the winner.

Teaching Tips: You may call out a question for which the teams must figure out the answer before forming the correct number.

Examples: How many points does a basket count?

How many points for a soccer goal?

How many points in a volleyball game?

You can also ask them to form letters.

Safety Tips

The players should have the opportunity to warm up and stretch before playing, to avoid injury. Also, do not let the players put any team member in a dangerous position.

40
PINBALL

Objectives: Catching, dodging, throwing

Players: Any number, equally divided into 2 teams

Equipment: A variety of sponge balls (12 or so), 6 plastic bowling pins

Playing Area: Gymnasium

Gross Motor Activity Rating: Good

Basic Skill Development Rating: Good

How to Play the Game: Each team scatters over its side of the gym floor. Behind them 3 bowling pins are arranged in a line.

At the start of the game the balls are randomly thrown onto the playing area, and 1 team tries to eliminate the other team by hitting opponents below shoulder level with thrown balls. If opponents catch the balls thrown at them, then the throwers are out and must go to the sidelines. However, when only 1 player is left from the team, and that player catches a thrown ball before getting hit, all of that player's teammates return to the playing area from the sidelines.

The object of the game is to be the first team to eliminate all opponents from the playing field and then to knock over the opponents' unprotected bowling pins to signify victory. The team that finishes first, wins.

Teaching Tips: If a bowling pin is accidentally knocked over before the team is eliminated, it should be placed upright by a player on the team.

Also, eliminated players stay the most active when they are put in a penalty area behind their opponents' pins. From that position they can try to recover tossed balls and throw them over their opponents' heads back to their own teammates. They must stay behind a line behind the pins and not come out to the playing field.

Safety Tips

Balls should be of the soft sponge variety, and players must not be allowed to aim at an opponent's head.

PLAYERS　　　　　　　　　　　PLAYERS

```
                    X              O
               X                 O
P                        X                        P
               X                    O
P                           X     O
               X                    O
P                                O
               X                    O
PINS                     X     O              PINS
```

41
PINBALL WIZARD

Objectives: Catching, dribbling, throwing, basketball skills

Players: 6-10 per team (2 teams)

Equipment: 2 Indian clubs, 2 balls (volleyball or soccer)

Playing Area: Gymnasium

Gross Motor Activity Rating: Excellent

Basic Skill Development Rating: Excellent

How to Play the Game: One goalie is assigned by each team to guard
the pin, and the remaining players spread out randomly on the floor. Each
team places its club in the center of the free throw circle. The goalie is
the only person allowed to enter that circle. The object of the game is
for the players to use dribbling and passing skills to knock over the guarded
pin.

The referee puts the 2 balls into play simultaneously by tossing them
into the air. The players pass and dribble, using the same basic skills as
in basketball, trying to work the ball toward the opponents' free throw
circle.

One point is awarded for each of the following:

- Knocking over the club with the ball
- Goalie accidentally knocking over the club
- Goalie holding or adjusting the club
- A player other than the goalie stepping into the circle
- Goalie stepping outside the circle

Teaching Tips: If a few players appear to be dominating the game, institute a rule that there must be a certain number of passes (each to a different person) before a throw at the pin may be attempted.

Safety Tips

Penalize teams for unnecessary roughness, such as pushing or personal-contact fouls.

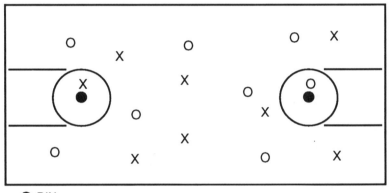

● PIN

42
222 PUNT & GO

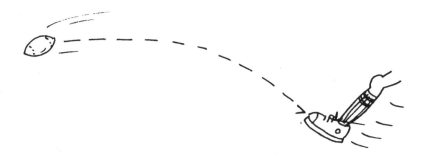

Objectives: Softball skills, running, throwing, catching

Players: 10 per team (2 teams)

Equipment: Floor tape for bases, foam football

Playing Area: Gymnasium

Gross Motor Activity Rating: Good

Basic Skill Development Rating: Good

How to Play the Game: Teams assume batting and fielding positions as in softball, with the exception that the batting team supplies the pitcher.

The game begins with the pitcher centering the ball to the first batter, who punts the ball into the field and then runs as in softball. No fielders are allowed in front of the pitcher until after the ball has been punted.

The fielding team can make an out by catching a fly ball or by throwing the batter out at a base as in softball.

One point is scored for each run by the batting team.

Teaching Tips: Divide the players into teams of equal strength.

For younger children you may use a round foam ball, which is easier to catch.

Safety Tips

Assess an automatic out if the batter kicks the ball at a fielder in a harmful manner.

43
RAT BALL

Objectives: Catching, running, throwing

Players: 10-15 per team (2 teams)

Equipment: Floor tape for bases, 1 foam ball, 2 cones

Playing Area: Gymnasium

Gross Motor Activity Rating: Good

Basic Skill Development Rating: Good

How to Play the Game: One team is lined up at the end of the gymnasium, and the other is scattered over the playing area—with 1 player designated as the pitcher, as shown in the diagram.

The game begins with the pitcher rolling the ball to the kicker, who kicks and then runs to first base. After the first pitch of an inning, the ball is always in play and the runners may run at any time.

An unlimited number of runners are allowed on base, and they may stay on a base as long as they like.

An out is called on the kicker if the kick does not go past the cones or if the kicked ball hits the ceiling.

The fielding team makes an out only by hitting the runner below the shoulders with the ball while the runner is off a base.

You may play 3 outs per team per inning or kick once through the batting orders.

One run is scored by each player who successfully makes 2 passes around the 4 bases.

Teaching Tips: Try to make the 2 teams equal.

Players should keep the ball moving rather than hold on to it and wait for a runner to go. The more runners on base, the easier it becomes to make an out.

Safety Tips

Penalize the fielding team for unnecessary roughness, such as interfering with the runners or throwing the balls too high.

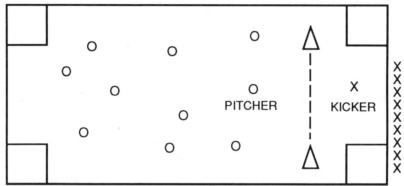

X TEAM OFFENSE

O TEAM DEFENSE

44
RAT TAIL RELAY

Objectives: Running

Players: 8-10 per team

Equipment: 1 rope and cone per team

Playing Area: Gymnasium

Gross Motor Activity Rating: Good

Basic Skill Development Rating: Fair

How to Play the Game: Divide the class into equal-sized teams. Each team lines up single file with each player holding on to the team's rope.

On the whistle the teams race down and around their cones and back across the finish line.

Teaching Tips: Variations could include walking backward, skipping, or hopping.

Safety Tips

Divide the players into teams of equal strength. Make sure the weaker students are not being pulled so that they fall.

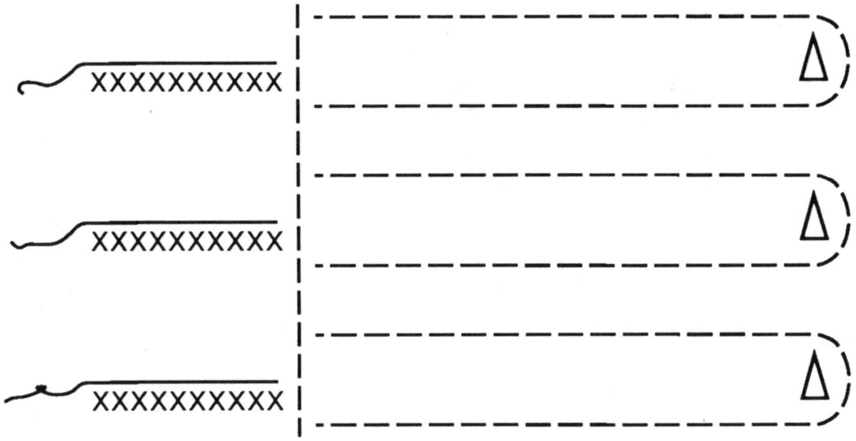
XXXXXXXXXX
XXXXXXXXXX
XXXXXXXXXX

45
RESCUE

Objectives: Problem solving

Players: Any even number per team (2 teams)

Equipment: 1 rope (about 5 feet long) for every player, pinnies

Playing Area: Gymnasium

Gross Motor Activity Rating: NA

Basic Skill Development Rating: NA

How to Play the Game: Divide the class into 2 teams, each team with its own color pinnie. Teammates pair up. Pairs of partners scatter around the gym and work only with each other.

One partner ties the ends of the rope to her or his wrists. The other partner does the same after looping the rope under the partner's rope.

The object of the game is to try to escape by untangling the 2 ropes without untying the knots or slipping the ropes off the wrists.

Once a pair figures it out, they run to their teammates (1 pair at a time) and show them how to untangle.

The first team to get all teammates untangled is the winner.

Teaching Tips: Be aware that some groups may figure the problem out very quickly and others may not figure it out even by the end of the class period.

Safety Tips

Be sure the students stretch properly before this activity because they will be bending and twisting.

Teacher's Clue

The partner with the lower rope makes a small loop with his or her rope and slides that loop under the rope on the partner's wrist, from the forearm toward the palm of the hand.

46
RULER OF THE SQUARES

Objectives: Catching, throwing

Players: 4-8 per large square

Equipment: Floor tape, 1 ball (playground, volleyball, or foam)

Playing Area: 14' square divided into 4 equal squares

Gross Motor Activity Rating: Fair

Basic Skill Development Rating: Good

How to Play the Game: One player is in each square; the remaining players line up alongside waiting to play, as shown in the diagram.

Play is started by the ruler dropping the ball to the floor and hitting it to the court diagonally opposite. The ball must hit the floor within that court and be hit on the first bounce to any other square.

The ball must not be returned to the square from which it came.

The ball may be hit with 1 or 2 hands, but it cannot be held or caught.

Players must have both feet in their squares whenever hitting the ball. When a player misses, he or she goes to the end of the waiting line, the first player in the waiting line moves into the number-4 square, and the remaining players move clockwise toward the ruler's square.

The player who can remain in the ruler's square the longest is the winner.

Teaching Tips: This game is thought of as an elementary game. However, older children can play and make it faster and more competitive.

Safety Tips

Remove any student from the squares who intentionally hits the ball at another student in a harmful manner.

RULER'S SQUARE 1 X	4 X
  2 X	 3 X

X X X X

47
RUN LIKE CRAZY RELAY

Objectives: Running, throwing

Players: 5-8 per team

Equipment: 4-6 hula hoops, 1 cone and 1 foam ball for every team

Playing Area: Gymnasium

Gross Motor Activity Rating: Good

Basic Skill Development Rating: Fair

How to Play the Game: Each team designates 1 player to be the thrower in the field. The remaining players are the runners and line up as shown in the diagram.

To start the game the first runner for each team throws a ball into the field (on your signal) and then runs around the cone and back to the line. The next player in line begins running as soon as the previous runner has returned.

The throwers may be anywhere in the field but must be inside a hula hoop before throwing a ball. The throwers try to hit any runner other than their teammate with a ball below the shoulders while the runner is running the course.

The throwers may run to retrieve a ball but must return to a hula hoop before throwing.

A team makes 1 point for every runner who makes it back safely. The team with the most points wins.

Teaching Tips: To run this relay more than once, rotate the throwers.

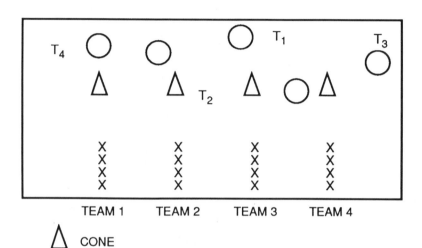

T_4 T_1 T_3 T_2

X	X	X	X
X	X	X	X
X	X	X	X
X	X	X	X
TEAM 1	TEAM 2	TEAM 3	TEAM 4

△ CONE

◯ HULA HOOP

48
RUNNERS & RAGGERS

Objectives: Catching, dribbling, shooting, basketball skills

Players: 10-15 per team (2 teams)

Equipment: Basketball

Playing Area: Basketball court

Gross Motor Activity Rating: Good

Basic Skill Development Rating: Excellent

How to Play the Game: Each team has 5 players on the court; the remaining players are on the sidelines.

The 10 court players play as in regulation basketball. The only exception is that a court player may pass only to a sideline player, and the sideline players pass to the court players.

Sideline players are not allowed to dribble and can hold the ball for only 5 seconds.

After 5 minutes the court players go to the end of the sideline and 5 new players take the court.

Scoring is the same as in basketball.

Teaching Tips: Divide the players into teams of equal strength.

Safety Tips

Penalize teams for unnecessary roughness, such as pushing or tripping.

49
SECRET AGENT "007"

Objectives: Dodging, running, throwing

Players: 10 per team (2 teams)

Equipment: 6 cones, 3-5 foam balls

Playing Area: Gymnasium

Gross Motor Activity Rating: Fair

Basic Skill Development Rating: Good

How to Play the Game: Divide the class into 2 equal teams, each team on its side of the playing area.

Each team chooses a "survivor" unknown to the other team.

The cones are set up in the center of the playing area to make a neutral zone as shown in the diagram. All players are allowed in the neutral zone, but none are allowed to cross into the opponents' area.

A player who is hit by a ball below the waist goes to a sideline and sits down. If the survivor touches a person who is sitting down, that player can resume playing. Once the survivor is hit, no player who has been eliminated can get back into the game.

A team is declared the winner when all of the opponents are sitting down.

Teaching Tips: Teammates may want to act as decoys by touching sitting players to confuse the opponents as to who is the real survivor.

Safety Tips

Penalize any student who throws the ball in a harmful manner at another student.

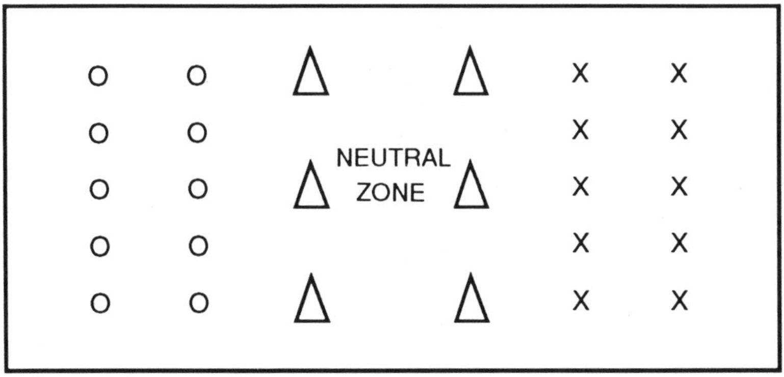
NEUTRAL
ZONE

50
SHOOT-OUT

Objectives: Running, shooting, stickhandling, hockey skills

Players: 10 per team (2 teams)

Equipment: Hockey sticks, foam puck, 1 portable hockey goal, 3 bowling pins

Playing Area: Gymnasium

Gross Motor Activity Rating: Fair

Basic Skill Development Rating: Good

How to Play the Game: Teams assume batting and fielding positions as in softball.

The first person up begins the game by hitting the puck into the field using a stationary hit with a hockey stick. The player then tries to run around all of the bases without stopping and get to home plate before the fielding team can score a goal.

The fielding team fields the puck and passes the puck to first, second, and third bases, knocking the pin down with the puck at each base. Once all the pins have been knocked down, the fielding team shoots the puck into the goal.

The fielders must use their sticks to pass the puck (no kicking of the puck is allowed). The player with possession of the puck is allowed only 2 steps before passing it.

If the runner gets home before the fielding team makes a goal, her or his team scores 1 point. If the fielding team finishes first, they score a point.

Teams switch after 1 time through the batting order.

Teaching Tips: After each point you may switch the fielders around so that more players will have a chance to play on a base.

If the fielders are having difficulty, you may need to make adjustments such as

- passing the puck to first, second, and third bases without having to knock down a pin,
- making the runner do 5 jumping jacks at each base,
- having the runner make 2 passes around the bases, or
- adding a goalie.

Safety Tips

Penalize any player who high-sticks or interferes with the base runner.

51
SKINK BALL

Objectives: Kicking, running

Players: 10-15 per team (2 teams)

Equipment: 1 tennis ball for every player, of a different color for each team

Playing Area: Gymnasium

Gross Motor Activity Rating: Good

Basic Skill Development Rating: Good

How to Play the Game:

Skink: A moving tennis ball

Splat: A stopped or dead ball

Sting: A penalty for a splat

All players are randomly spaced throughout the playing area. Four officials are spread out over the gym.

The game begins by an official rolling all the skinks onto the gym floor.

Each team tries to keep all of its skinks moving by kicking them around the gym. A player may move anywhere in the gym but is not allowed to pick up or throw the skinks. Players may stop the opponents' skinks with their feet but must immediately take their feet off them.

The 4 officials are on the lookout for splats. When an official spots a splat, she or he awards a sting to the appropriate team. It is legal for players to a point out to the officials any splats they see.

If an official spots the splat before the team is able to kick it back into play, a sting is awarded.

Whenever a team has been awarded 10 stings, it loses that game or round.

Teaching Tips: Keep track of the number of stings awarded to each team.

This game may also be played for a set time with the team having the fewest stings being the winner.

Safety Tips

Penalize any player who kicks the balls too hard or in a harmful manner.

52
SNOW RUGBY

Objectives: Running, catching, throwing

Players: 10-40 (2 teams)

Equipment: Foam football, pinnies to distinguish players, whistle, cones or tape to mark the goal line

Playing Area: Gymnasium or outdoor field

Gross Motor Activity Rating: Excellent

Basic Skill Development Rating: Fair

How to Play the Game: The 2 teams have equal numbers of players, randomly scattered throughout the field. The game is similar to Hot Potato.

The game begins with a whistle and a ball tossed up from the center of the playing area. The team who gains possession begins toward the goal line. The player running with the ball must toss the ball up in the air or pass it to a teammate with every whistle, but the pass must not be more than a 10-yard distance.

An interception from the opponents turns the game to the opposite direction. The referee shall blow the whistle as often as every 5 to 10 seconds.

A ball carried across the goal line scores 2 points. A ball passed and caught by a teammate in the goal area scores 1 point. No offsides are called, and a passed goal is legal if at least 2 opponents are also in the goal area.

The game is resumed after a goal with a tossed ball in the center of the gym.

Teaching Tips: The game is very active and is played best if absolutely no passes are allowed to be thrown more than 10 yards. The game is great fun outdoors in snow, also!

Safety Tips

No contact is allowed. The opponents gain possession of the ball on a violation, or the individual called on violation may be asked to sit out for a misconduct penalty. Do not allow any unnecessary roughness.

53
SPEEDY SNEAKIES

Objectives: Catching, throwing

Players: 6-12 per team (2 teams)

Equipment: 8'' foam ball, 2 goals marked by floor tape or cones

Playing Area: Gymnasium

Gross Motor Activity Rating: Excellent

Basic Skill Development Rating: Excellent

How to Play the Game: The teams have equal numbers of players on the court and 1 player each in the goal. Players must stay on their sides of the midcourt line during play.

The game begins with a jump ball.

The goal area can be the mat often found on the gymnasium wall behind each basket, or it could be an area approximately 6 feet long marked off by floor tape or cones.

The ball is passed from player to player. When a teammate catches the ball, he or she may take no more than 2 steps before passing the ball to another teammate. The ball cannot be kicked.

Defense and offense cannot cross the halfcourt line. After a goal is scored, the goalie puts the ball in play by passing the ball into the court to a defensive player.

A goal is scored when the ball is thrown and hits the goal area or goes between the cones.

Teaching Tips: The game is played best if all players continually pass and try to advance the ball. There should be no stalling. The ball could be turned over to the opponents if there is a delay of more than 10 seconds. The penalty for unsportsmanlike play should be a 1-minute penalty, which would give the opponents a 1-player advantage.

If a few players seem to dominate play, you may institute a rule that at least 2 girls and 2 boys must come in contact with the ball before an attempt to score is made.

Safety Tips

This is a noncontact game and is played in a fashion similar to basketball. No roughness is allowed.

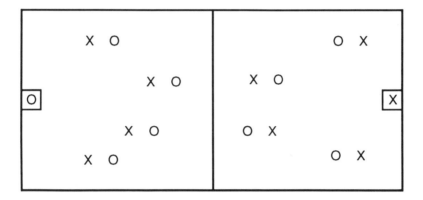

54
SPIDER'S WEB

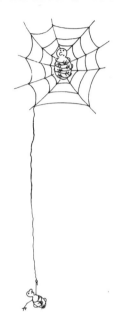

Objectives: Problem solving

Players: Minimum of 10

Equipment: None

Playing Area: Gymnasium

Gross Motor Activity Rating: NA

Basic Skill Development Rating: NA

How to Play the Game: Everyone begins by forming a single line. Call for all players to cross their hands and then join hands with the 2 players on either side of them.

Then give instructions to twist the line, turn, circle, and have the 2 end players go under and through various breaks in the line. When a tangled web appears and you are satisfied by its complexity, give the signal for the players to try to untangle without breaking the line.

Teaching Tips: Two or more groups doing the same thing could have a contest to see who untangles the fastest! Or allow 1 group to see how tangled they can make their opponents be!

Safety Tips

Players should hang onto each other's hands but not twist.

55
SQUARE-OFF RELAY

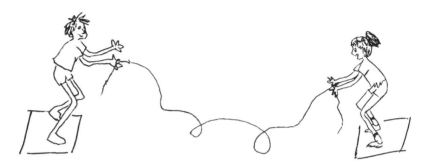

Objectives: Dodging

Players: 2 equal teams of about 6 per team

Equipment: 1 rope about 30' or longer, floor tape to mark 1' squares

Playing Area: Gymnasium

Gross Motor Activity Rating: Good

Basic Skill Development Rating: Good

How to Play the Game: Each team begins with players lined up behind the square at that team's end of the rope. One rope is needed for 2 groups.

Position the squares so that there is approximately 10 feet of slack in the ropes.

The first person in line steps into the square and holds the end of the rope (all the slack should be in the middle).

At the sound of the whistle, the first 2 opposing players pull up the slack and try to pull each other off the square. When all of the slack is out of the rope, a player can either pull on the rope or let up to cause the opponent to become off-balance and step out of the square. When a player steps out of the square, the next person steps in to challenge the winner. No one is allowed to help the 2 players.

Whichever team outlasts its opponents is the winner!

Teaching Tips: If 1 foot comes out of the square, the player loses and the next player steps forward into the square.

Safety Tips

Make sure both players are ready before blowing the whistle to begin. Encourage players to start in a steady, feet-apart, knees-bent position.

56
STRANDED RELAY

Objectives: Problem solving

Players: 10 per team

Equipment: 20'' square area, marked off by floor tape—one for each team

Playing Area: Small portion of gymnasium

Gross Motor Activity Rating: NA

Basic Skill Development Rating: NA

How to Play the Game: Divide the group into equal teams of about 10 people each. Each team will have its own taped square. The size of the group determines how big the taped square will be.

At the sound of the whistle, each team must try to figure out a way to get all its teammates together on the taped square and remain there for 30 seconds.

The group to accomplish this fastest is the winner. This is a problem-solving activity, so each team must find their own solution.

Teaching Tips: This will take some group effort. Prepare the group by explaining this ahead of time.

Safety Tips

Explain to the players that they must hold on to each other and maintain balance so no injuries are incurred.

57
SWEEPSTAKES

Objectives: Running, shooting, stickhandling

Players: 10-15 per team (2 teams)

Equipment: Volleyball, 12 brooms, 4 cones

Playing Area: Gymnasium

Gross Motor Activity Rating: Good

Basic Skill Development Rating: Good

How to Play the Game: Each team lines up on its designated sideline with the brooms lying near the end lines as shown in the diagram.

The game begins with 5 players from each team running onto the field, picking up their brooms, and attempting to hit the ball through the opponents' goal.

The goalies are the only persons allowed to touch the ball with their hands. The brooms must not be raised off the floor.

After 3 minutes of play or after a goal, the 10 players on the court return the brooms to the end lines and go to the end of their teams' lines. On the whistle the next 5 from each team play.

One point is scored each time a goal is scored.

Teaching Tips: If the teams are too large, play 2 games crosscourt.

You may include the sideline players by allowing them goalie privileges.

Safety Tips

Penalize any student who high-sticks or shows unnecessary roughness, such as pushing or tripping.

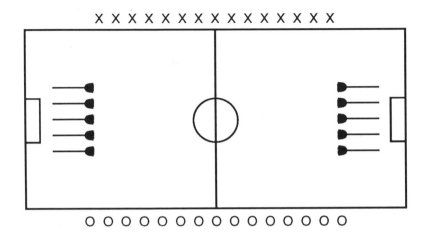

58
TEAM TOSS

Objectives: Catching, throwing

Players: 6 per team

Equipment: Badminton net and standards, Frisbee or large beanbag

Playing Area: Gymnasium

Gross Motor Activity Rating: Good

Basic Skill Development Rating: Fair

How to Play the Game: Teams assume positions on the court as for volleyball.

The person in the serving position begins the game with an underhand throw to the opponents, who attempt to catch the Frisbee and throw it back across the net.

Play continues until the Frisbee hits the floor or until a throw goes into the net.

Scoring is the same as in volleyball. A team can score only if it is serving and wins the volley. The first team to score 15 points is the winner.

Teaching Tips: You may want to use a lower net and a beanbag for younger elementary children.

Safety Tips

Penalize any player who throws the Frisbee in a harmful manner at another player.

59
TEAM TRIVIA

Objectives: Cognitive learning

Players: Any number, equally divided into 2 teams

Equipment: 5 cones or bases per team, sport trivia questions or sport rules questions

Playing Area: Small room

Gross Motor Activity Rating: NA

Basic Skill Development Rating: NA

How to Play the Game: Divide the class into 2 equal teams. Act as the game host. Teams alternate answering questions and either number off or sit in a row to keep in order. The object of the game is to correctly answer as many questions as possible.

Line up a row of 5 cones in front of each team. Player Number 1 from the first team is asked a question. If she or he answers correctly, the player moves to the first cone. The second question goes to the opposing team, and further questions continue to alternate between the 2 teams.

If the second player answers the given question correctly for the team, that player goes to the first cone and the player that was at the first cone now moves to the second cone. The team whose teammates advance first to the 5th cone wins that round.

Players may consult with teammates for answers, but if any answer is incorrect, the farthest-advanced player on the team is backed up 1 place.

Teaching Tips: Allow each player a set length of time to answer his or her question. The first answer given by the player whose turn it is, is the answer accepted. Allow each team the same number of questions as its opponents; make sure that the team that began second gets its chance at its last question.

The following are samples of sport trivia questions. Adapt your own questions for the activity your students are learning.

1. What is the award given to the outstanding college football player each year?
   (*Heismann Trophy*)

2. Fishing is also called what?
   (*Angling*)

3. Which horse race is known as the Run for the Roses?
   (*Kentucky Derby*)

4. Name the basketball team that is the unofficial ambassador of sport and clowning?
   (*Harlem Globetrotters*)

5. The Stanley Cup is associated with what sport?
   (*Ice hockey*)

6. In what sport might you be caught in a suicide squeeze?
   (*Baseball*)

7. Why did the golfer only wear 1 shoe?
   (*Because he had a hole in 1*)

8. In what sport is love a real zero?
   (*Tennis*)

9. In what country was the first Olympics held?
   (*Greece*)

10. What sport uses clowns to protect its competitors?
    (*Rodeo*)

11. What's the first instruction given runners by the starter of a race?
    (*On your mark*)

12. What sport has you herringboning to get up a hill?
    (*Skiing*)

13. Who stopped Bjorn Borg's string of Wimbledon singles titles at 5?
    (*John McEnroe*)

14. What's another term for a badminton bird?
    (*Shuttlecock*)

15. How many points are awarded for a safety in football?
    (*2*)

16. How many innings are there in a regulation softball game?
    (*7*)
17. What was originally called the Pluto Plater?
    (*The Frisbee*)
18. How many players are there on a soccer team?
    (*11*)
19. How many bowling balls does it take to make a spare?
    (*2*)
20. What sport is played in more countries than any other?
    (*Soccer*)
21. Who was *Sports Illustrated*'s first Sportswoman of the Year?
    (*Billie Jean King*)
22. How many Olympic medals has gymnast Cathy Rigby won?
    (*Zero*)
23. What nonmechanical sport achieves the highest speed?
    (*Skydiving*)
24. What was the biggest-selling toy of 1957?
    (*Hula hoop*)
25. What is an expert rifle shooter called?
    (*A marksman*)
26. What's the back boundary line in tennis called?
    (*Baseline*)
27. What sport uses the term "double axel"?
    (*Figure skating*)
28. What zone varies from batter to batter in baseball?
    (*Strike zone*)
29. What is the national sport of Japan?
    (*Sumo wrestling*)
30. What ball game did James Naismith invent at Springfield, Massachusetts?
    (*Basketball*)
31. What sport do you throw bombs in?
    (*Football*)
32. What vehicles are raced in the Tour de France?
    (*Bicycles*)
33. What is a perfect score in gymnastic exercise?
    (*10*)

34. What kind of surface are the Wimbledon tennis championships played on?
    (*Grass*)

35. What is the only major sport that allows substitutions while play is in progress?
    (*Hockey*)

36. What is the fastest stroke in swimming?
    (*Front crawl or freestyle*)

37. What is a turkey in bowling?
    (*3 consecutive strikes*)

38. What is the tennis term for missing on first and second serves?
    (*Double fault*)

39. What has 336 dimples?
    (*Golf ball*)

40. What Olympic event's winner is considered the world's greatest athlete?
    (*Decathlon*)

41. What pro sport did Wilt Chamberlin play after basketball?
    (*Volleyball*)

42. What number wood is the driver in golf?
    (*1*)

43. In football, how many yards do you need to get for a first down?
    (*10*)

44. In table tennis, how many points do you need to win?
    (*21*)

45. How many times may a volleyball team hit the ball before it must go over the net?
    (*3*)

46. What is the name of the NBA basketball team from Dallas?
    (*Mavericks*)

47. In what sport do you have a shortstop?
    (*Baseball*)

48. When Henry Aaron broke the all-time home-run record, whose record did he break?
    (*Babe Ruth's*)

49. Can you dribble a ball in soccer?
    (*Yes*)

50. How many players on 1 team can be on a volleyball court at a time?
    (*6*)

51. In basketball, what is the call if you run with the ball without dribbling?
    (*Traveling*)

52. Will a regular aerobic exercise program increase or decrease your resting heart rate?
    (*Decrease*)

53. What type of stretch will increase flexibility?
    (*Static stretch*)

54. Your heart should be worked at what percent of its heart-rate capacity during aerobics to obtain results?
    (*65 to 80 percent*)

55. In badminton what is any violation of the rules called?
    (*Fault*)

56. In badminton an offensive shot hit hard downward toward the ground is called what?
    (*Smash*)

57. In badminton, can both the servers and receivers score, depending on who wins the rally?
    (*No*)

58. In badminton must the serve be an underhand stroke?
    (*Yes*)

60
THREE-POINTER RELAY

Objectives: Problem solving

Players: Several teams of 5-7 per team

Equipment: None

Playing Area: Gymnasium

Gross Motor Activity Rating: Excellent

Basic Skill Development Rating: Fair

How to Play the Game: Each team has 5 to 7 members. If the team has 5 members, use 3 points of contact with the floor; if the team has 7 members, use 4 or 5 points of contact for the challenge.

The object of the relay is to get all players across the gym using only the number of total contact points allowed.

Teaching Tips: Explain that no single way is the right way and that creativity and group effort will help solve the challenge. It is best solved taking time to decide how to move rather than hurrying and falling apart!

Safety Tips

Check to see that the group appears to be stable and balanced before allowing the group to begin.

Do not allow any player to be placed in a dangerous position.

61
TIC-TAC VOLLEY

Objectives: Volleyball skills

Players: 5-8 per team (4 teams)

Equipment: 4 volleyball nets, 5 standards, 1 volleyball

Playing Area: Gymnasium space to accommodate 2 nets side by side

Gross Motor Activity Rating: Fair

Basic Skill Development Rating: Excellent

How to Play the Game: Each team spreads out to best cover its court, as shown in the diagram.

The game begins by any back-row player serving to anyone on the other 3 courts. Players may return the ball to any court.

Regulation volleyball rules apply except for scoring. Points are scored against a team for missing a serve, hitting a ball out of bounds, or letting the ball hit the floor on the team's court.

Service is taken by the team that ended up with the ball at the end of the volley.

The game is played to 15 points, at which time the team with the lowest score wins the game. If 2 teams are tied for low score, a play-off continues between them until the tie is broken.

Teaching Tips: It is helpful to have an official and a scorer.

Safety Tips

Players must be alert at all times because they never know when the ball may be hit into their courts.

```
         O       O     O        X       X       X
            O       O                 X       X
         O     O       O        X       X       X

NET ┌──────────────────────┬──────────────────────┐
     Z     Z     Z          V       V       V
        Z       Z                 V       V
     Z     Z     Z          V       V       V
```

NET

62
TOSS-CATCH BASKET RELAY

Objectives: Catching, throwing

Players: 4-6 per team

Equipment: 1 ball and 1 bucket per team

Playing Area: Gymnasium

Gross Motor Activity Rating: Fair

Basic Skill Development Rating: Good

How to Play the Game: Each team lines up behind the start line. One tosser from each team stands behind another line about 20 feet away from the start line.

The first person in each line holds the bucket and steps up to the line to catch. The tosser lobs the ball to the catcher, who attempts to catch the ball in the bucket without stepping over the line. If it's a miss, the catcher throws the ball back to the tosser and they go again.

When the ball is caught, the catcher takes the ball out of the bucket and runs to become the next tosser. The first tosser runs to the end of the team's line. The new tosser lobs the ball to the next person in line.

The first team to have everyone catch a ball is the winner.

Teaching Tips: The distance between the 2 lines may need to be adjusted according to the age and skill levels of the players.

Safety Tips

Do not allow any aggressive play.

63

TRIPLE CROWN BASEBALL

Objectives: Softball skills, running, throwing, catching

Players: 10-15 per team (2 teams)

Equipment: Floor tape for bases, a variety of balls (football, foam, playground, tennis, Frisbee), a trashcan or box

Playing Area: Gymnasium or baseball field

Gross Motor Activity Rating: Good

Basic Skill Development Rating: Good

How to Play the Game: One team is lined up in the batting position, and the other team is scattered randomly in the field with at least 1 player positioned at the basket. The balls are all in a box at home plate.

The first batter comes to the plate and selects 3 balls of any kind. The batter throws or kicks the 3 balls into the field and then attempts to run around all of the bases and back to home.

The fielding team attempts to field all 3 balls and return them to the basket before the runner can get home.

A caught fly ball does not have to be returned to the basket.

A runner making it all the way home scores 4 points. A runner making it to third base scores 3 points, to second base 2 points, and to first base 1 point. Runners left on base are awarded the appropriate number of points and then return to the end of the batting line.

When everyone on the team has had a turn, the teams trade places.

Teaching Tips: If the teams have enough players to cover the field sufficiently, it is better to have 2 players standing at the basket to catch the balls. Rotate the players at the basket often.

Safety Tips

Penalize the fielding team with an automatic 4 points for the batting team if the runner is in any way interfered with.

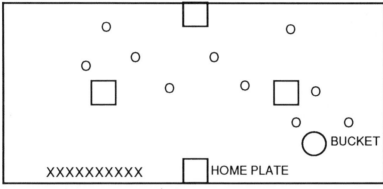

64
VOLLEYBALL PLUS

Objectives: Volleyball skills

Players: 6 per team (2 teams)

Equipment: Volleyball, net, standards

Playing Area: Gymnasium

Gross Motor Activity Rating: Excellent

Basic Skill Development Rating: Excellent

How to Play the Game: Each team begins the game with 6 players. The game begins after a volley for serve.

Regulation volleyball is played, except for scoring. Each team can score either 1 point or 3 points when it has control of the serve. Once the ball in play is returned to the serving team, the official may announce "Bonus." Then if the serving team executes 3 legal hits before the ball crosses over the net, they win 3 bonus points. If "Bonus" is not announced and they win the rally, only 1 regulation point is counted. Any intentional failure to return the serve so the serving team could not be in bonus is not allowed.

This game encourages ball control skills and teamwork. Using 2 referees is helpful. The game is over when 1 team reaches 15 points.

Teaching Tips: A variation of the game might be to allow both teams to score. Every legal hit up to 3 per side could count regardless of who has served. Two officials should be used to tally points and referee.

Safety Tips

Call fouls, at the net particularly, to avoid rough play.

65
VOLLEYSOCK

Objectives: Soccer skills

Players: 4-8 per team (2 teams)

Equipment: 1 volleyball net and standards, 1 dense foam ball

Playing Area: Gymnasium

Gross Motor Activity Rating: Fair

Basic Skill Development Rating: Excellent

How to Play the Game: Five players from each team position themselves on the court, and the remaining players line up on the side.

The game begins with an underhand, easy lob serve to the other team. The receiving team has 4 hits plus 1 bounce to return the ball across the net. All hits must consist of kicking or heading the ball as in soccer.

At the end of every volley each team rotates in a new player.

Scoring is the same as in volleyball.

Teaching Tips: This game is for students who have more advanced soccer skills.

If your gym space allows, you may want to use more courts so that no players are waiting to rotate in.

Safety Tips

Emphasis must be placed on controlled soccer skills and not kicking the ball too hard.

66
WHEEL OF TORTURE

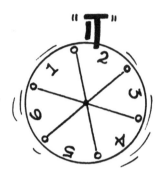

Objectives: Running

Players: Groups of 5-7

Equipment: None

Playing Area: Gymnasium or outdoor play area

Gross Motor Activity Rating: Excellent

Basic Skill Development Rating: NA

How to Play the Game: The group is divided into smaller groups of 5 to 7 players. The object of the game is to prevent the player who is "it" from tagging a designated player in the group.

One player is designated as "it" and the remaining players join hands to form a circle with the "it" player on the outside. "It" tries to tag a designated member of the circle. The circle of players is continuously moving, trying to prevent the tag from happening. "It" must stay on the outside of the circle. Once tagged the designated player is now "it."

Teaching Tips: Divide players into groups of similar strengths. This is a fast-moving, fun game requiring fast footwork.

Safety Tips

Do not allow weaker players to be dragged around.
Modify to accommodate players.

67
YOU'RE HOT YOU'RE HOT!

Objectives: Running

Players: 10-15 per team (2 teams)

Equipment: Dixie cups, water source, 2 or more buckets, a hot day

Playing Area: Outdoor playground

Gross Motor Activity Rating: Good

Basic Skill Development Rating: Poor

How to Play the Game: Divide the players into 2 teams.

Each team member has a dixie cup and gets water from the water source, which may either be a faucet or a bucket of water. All players fill their dixie cups, run to dump the water into their team's buckets, then run back to refill their cups.

After the designated time is up, the team with the most water in its bucket is the winner.

Teaching Tips: If you have a large number of players you may want to use 2 buckets for water sources.

```
┌─────────────────────────────────────────────┐
│                 Safety Tips                   │
│  No player contact is allowed.                │
│     Be watchful for slippery surfaces—a grassy area │
│  works well.                                  │
└─────────────────────────────────────────────┘
```

68
WOLF'S DEN

Objectives: Running, stickhandling, hockey skills

Players: 6-12 per team (2 teams)

Equipment: Hockey sticks, puck, 1-3 plastic bowling pins, floor tape

Playing Area: Gymnasium

Gross Motor Activity Rating: Fair

Basic Skill Development Rating: Good

How to Play the Game: Teams assume batting and fielding positions as in softball.

The first player in the batting line hits the puck into the field and tries to run around to all of the dens and home again. The dens are squares taped on the wall, and the runner must touch each one.

The fielding team must get the puck and knock down all the pins with the puck before the runner gets home. The fielder with the puck must not run with it, but rather must pass it to another fielder who is closer to the pins.

It is important to have the fielders strategically placed throughout the field with at least 2 players close to the pins, because passing the puck from player to player is the only way to move the puck to the pins.

The pins may be knocked down only with the puck.

When everyone on the batting team has run, they become the fielding team.

If the base runner makes it home before the pins are knocked down, the batting team scores 1 point. If the fielding team knocks the pins over before the runner gets home, the fielding team scores 1 point.

Teaching Tips: For younger or less skilled students you may want to use only 1 bowling pin.

Divide the players into teams of equal strength.
Make sure the game ends with a completed inning.

Safety Tips

Penalize players for high-sticking or interfering with
base runners.

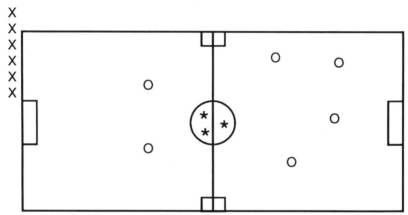

STAND PINS ANYWHERE IN MIDDLE OF CIRCLE

★ PINS

X OFFENSE

O DEFENSE

69
ZONEY BALL

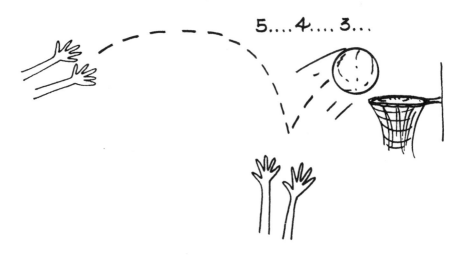

5.... 4.... 3...

Objectives: Shooting, basketball skills

Players: 8-12 per team (2 teams)

Equipment: Basketballs, floor tape to mark end zone

Playing Area: Gymnasium with basketball hoops

Gross Motor Activity Rating: Excellent

Basic Skill Development Rating: Excellent

How to Play the Game: The 2 teams have equal numbers of players on the court and in the end zone.

The game begins with a jump ball. Fielders of both teams try to gain possession of the ball. The fielders may move about center court with the same privileges as a basketball team and attempt to pass the ball to a "zoney" (an end-zone player). The ball must be caught by a zoney, who cannot leave the end-zone area. The end-zone player must attempt to shoot a basket within 5 seconds. If the player misses the basket, she or he must toss the ball back to the fielders. Fielders from either team are eligible to gain possession of the tossed ball. A point is scored each time a zoney player successfully shoots the ball into the basket.

Teaching Tips: Rotate players' positions during the game to encourage skill development in both passing and shooting.

Encourage players to pass the ball at least once to another fielder before a pass to the end zone is made.

The game could be played in a halfcourt playing area to accommodate more players.

Safety Tips

This is a noncontact game with lead-up skills for basketball. No pushing, shoving, or reaching in to guard an opponent is allowed.

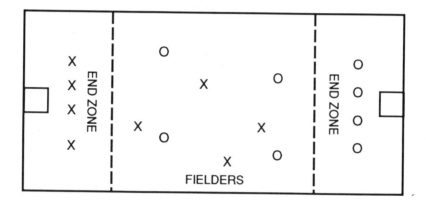

About the Authors

Marilee Gustafson is a secondary physical education and health teacher at Anoka (MN) Senior High School. She has also been responsible for developing a curriculum for group games at Anoka Hennepin District #11. Marilee, who has taught since 1969 and coached through 1981, was nominated as Minnesota's Physical Educator of the Year in 1989. In her spare time, she enjoys family outings, dance, and biking.

Sue Wolfe has been a physical education instructor at Anoka Senior High School since 1976. Sue realized the great need for a book like *Great Games for Young People* when she took charge of developing the curriculum for a games unit at Anoka. Over the years, she has been a guest instructor of games presentations and a curriculum developer for large-group game instruction. In her leisure, Sue enjoys golf, biking, and traveling.

Cheryl King has been the head tennis and track coach at Anoka Senior High School since 1976. She taught junior high physical education and health at Jackson Junior High in Champlin and Coon Rapids Junior High from 1970 to 1979. She has also been a park and recreation instructor for youth basketball, soccer, and baseball. King was nominated as Minnesota State High School Coach of the Year in 1982 and is president of the Minnesota State High School Tennis Association. In her leisure, King enjoys tennis, golf, fishing, and hunting.